## Praise for *Proven Portals*

This book is chock-full of valuable knowledge and practical advice on implementing portals. Dan Sullivan once again gives us comprehensive information and useful techniques for delivering what's become a business staple. A must-read for practitioners and managers alike!

—Jill Dyché, Partner, Baseline Consulting Group

Enterprise portals are a key component in supporting enterprise business integration, and this book is a must-read for anyone involved in planning or deploying a portal solution.

—Colin White, President, Intelligent Business Strategies

Enterprise portals have moved from the fringes of business to a core competency in the span of a few short years. This book provides the balanced overview managers need to make intelligent decisions without dragging them into a morass of technical detail.

—Marcia Robinson, President, E-Business Strategies
Author of *Services Blueprint: Roadmap for Execution*

Portals have become the ubiquitous format for most uses of the Web. If you are venturing into portal land, whether for the first time or after a few experiences, Dan Sullivan's book, *Proven Portals: Best Practices for Planning, Designing, and Developing Enterprise Portals,* is a valuable guide for getting organized and oriented. Understanding the approaches, technologies, and best practices described in this book will help ensure that your portal project is both a technical and a business success.

—Rose O'Donnell, Vice President of Engineering, Bowstreet, Inc.

# Proven Portals

# Addison-Wesley Information Technology Series
## Capers Jones and David S. Linthicum, Consulting Editors

The information technology (IT) industry is in the public eye now more than ever before because of a number of major issues in which software technology and national policies are closely related. As the use of software expands, there is a continuing need for business and software professionals to stay current with the state of the art in software methodologies and technologies. The goal of the **Addison-Wesley Information Technology Series** is to cover any and all topics that affect the IT community. These books illustrate and explore how information technology can be aligned with business practices to achieve business goals and support business imperatives. Addison-Wesley has created this innovative series to empower you with the benefits of the industry experts' experience.

For more information point your browser to www.awprofessional.com/itseries

Sid Adelman, Larissa Terpeluk Moss, *Data Warehouse Project Management.* ISBN: 0-201-61635-1

Sid Adelman et al., *Impossible Data Warehouse Situations: Solutions from the Experts.* ISBN: 0-201-76033-9

Wayne Applehans, Alden Globe, and Greg Laugero, *Managing Knowledge: A Practical Web-Based Approach.* ISBN: 0-201-43315-X

David Leon Clark, *Enterprise Security: The Manager's Defense Guide.* ISBN: 0-201-71972-X

Frank P. Coyle, *XML, Web Services, and the Data Revolution.* ISBN: 0-201-77641-3

Kevin Dick, *XML, Second Edition: A Manager's Guide.* ISBN: 0-201-77006-7

Jill Dyché, *e-Data: Turning Data into Information with Data Warehousing.* ISBN: 0-201-65780-5

Jill Dyché, *The CRM Handbook: A Business Guide to Customer Relationship Management.* ISBN: 0-201-73062-6

Patricia L. Ferdinandi, *A Requirements Pattern: Succeeding in the Internet Economy.* ISBN: 0-201-73826-0

David Garmus and David Herron, *Function Point Analysis: Measurement Practices for Successful Software Projects.* ISBN: 0-201-69944-3

John Harney, *Application Service Providers (ASPs): A Manager's Guide.* ISBN: 0-201-72659-9

International Function Point Users Group, *IT Measurement: Practical Advice from the Experts.* ISBN: 0-201-74158-X

Capers Jones, *Software Assessments, Benchmarks, and Best Practices.* ISBN: 0-201-48542-7

Ravi Kalakota and Marcia Robinson, *e-Business 2.0: Roadmap for Success.* ISBN: 0-201-72165-1

Ravi Kalakota and Marcia Robinson, *Services Blueprint: Roadmap for Execution.* ISBN: 0-321-15039-2

Greg Laugero and Alden Globe, *Enterprise Content Services: Connecting Information and Profitability.* ISBN: 0-201-73016-2

David S. Linthicum, *B2B Application Integration: e-Business-Enable Your Enterprise.* ISBN: 0-201-70936-8

David S. Linthicum, *Enterprise Application Integration.* ISBN: 0-201-61583-5

David S. Linthicum, *Next Generation Application Integration: From Simple Information to Web Services.* ISBN: 0-201-84456-7

Sergio Lozinsky, *Enterprise-Wide Software Solutions: Integration Strategies and Practices.* ISBN: 0-201-30971-8

Anne Thomas Manes, *Web Services: A Manager's Guide.* ISBN: 0-321-18577-3

Larissa T. Moss and Shaku Atre, *Business Intelligence Roadmap: The Complete Project Lifecycle for Decision-Support Applications.* ISBN: 0-201-78420-3

Bud Porter-Roth, *Request for Proposal: A Guide to Effective RFP Development.* ISBN: 0-201-77575-1

Ronald G. Ross, *Principles of the Business Rule Approach.* ISBN: 0-201-78893-4

Dan Sullivan, *Proven Portals: Best Practices for Planning, Designing, and Developing Enterprise Portals.* ISBN: 0-321-12520-7

Karl E. Wiegers, *Peer Reviews in Software: A Practical Guide.* ISBN: 0-201-73485-0

Ralph R. Young, *Effective Requirements Practices.* ISBN: 0-201-70912-0

Bill Zoellick, *CyberRegs: A Business Guide to Web Property, Privacy, and Patents.* ISBN: 0-201-72230-5

# Proven Portals

## Best Practices for Planning, Designing, and Developing Enterprise Portals

**Dan Sullivan**

✦✦ Addison-Wesley

Boston • San Francisco • New York • Toronto • Montreal
London • Munich • Paris • Madrid
Capetown • Sydney • Tokyo • Singapore • Mexico City

The publisher offers discounts on this book when ordered in quantity for bulk purchases and special sales. For more information, please contact:

> U.S. Corporate and Government Sales
> (800) 382-3419
> corpsales@pearsontechgroup.com

For sales outside of the U.S., please contact:

> International Sales
> (317) 581-3793
> international@pearsontechgroup.com

Visit Addison-Wesley on the Web: www.awprofessional.com

*Library of Congress Cataloging-in-Publication Data*

Sullivan, Dan, 1962–
　　Proven portals best practices for planning, designing, and developing
enterprise portals / Dan Sullivan
　　　　p.　cm.
　　Includes bibliographical references and index.
　　ISBN 0-321-12520-7 (pbk. : alk. paper)
　　1. Web Portals—Design.　2. Web site development.　3. Business enterprises—
Computer networks.　I. Title.
　　TK5105.888.S82　2003
　　025.04—dc21　　　　　　　　　　　　　　　　　　2003012061

ISBN 0-321-12520-7
Text printed on recycled paper
1 2 3 4 5 6 7 8 9 10 — CRS — 0706050403
First printing, September 2003

*To Jane and Bill*

# Contents

# PART I  Principles of Portal Design

### CHAPTER 1  CREATING FRAMEWORKS FOR ORGANIZING INFORMATION  3

### CHAPTER 2  USING A THREE-TIER ARCHITECTURE  25

CHAPTER 3  **USING A FRAMEWORK FOR APPLICATION INTEGRATION  43**

CHAPTER 4  **ENSURING PORTAL ADOPTION  63**

| CHAPTER 5 | **MEASURING PORTAL RETURN ON INVESTMENT: A CRASH COURSE** **81** |
|---|---|

# PART II  The Variety of Portals

# PART III   Building Your Own Proven Portal

## CHAPTER 9   FIVE COMMON THEMES IN PROVEN PORTALS   163

## CHAPTER 10   IMPLEMENTING YOUR PROVEN PORTAL   171

# Case Studies

# List of Figures

# Preface

If you need to plan, design, or deploy an enterprise portal this book is for you. Initiating a portal project (or rescuing one under way) is an exciting, sometimes daunting, challenge. Fortunately, the craft of portal design is now mature enough to identify the best practices that lead to successful implementations. Examples of those implementations, or proven portals, and detailed discussions of design principals are provided throughout this book.

Part I discusses several elements of portal design, including:

- Organizing information in an intuitive, coherent manner
- Creating a modular, adaptable framework for application integration
- Identifying core portal services, such as collaboration and content management
- Developing a robust, scalable architecture

These technical topics are complemented by organizational issues that should be addressed early in the life of a portal, specifically, ensuring adoption by end users and assessing the financial benefits of the portal.

Part II examines details particular to three common application areas: customer service, business intelligence, and knowledge management.

Part III summarizes core principles of successful portals and provides a guide to developing your own enterprise portal.

Creating an enterprise portal is a challenging and rewarding experience. With a solid understanding of your business requirements and knowledge of the best practices found in this book, you are well positioned to create your own proven portal.

# Acknowledgments

Books have many authors, although few names appear on the cover. This one is no exception. *Proven Portals* is the product of colleagues choosing to share their insights, editors capable of shaping a raw manuscript into a finished product, and, most importantly, a family willing to put up with the whole process.

No one person's experience can create a book like this, and I am indebted to my colleagues who shared their hard-earned experiences that constitute some of the best practices in portal design and development. I would like to thank Gerard van der Burg of the Global Development Group; Lisa Dekker and Margaret Dobbin of Open Text; Trudy Dunham of the University of Minnesota; Jayne Dutra and Jeanne Holm of the NASA Jet Propulsion Laboratory; David Gerger and Chris Kneeland of Center Partners; Paul Hamnett of the Institute for Healthcare Improvement; Doug Greenfield of Plumtree; Andy Hackbarth of October East Associates; Shelly Hayduk and Harlan Hugh of TheBrain Technologies Corporation; Kenny Klepper of Empire Blue Cross Blue Shield; Dr. Ganapathy Krishnan of MusicNet; Brandon Lackey of Halliburton; Judy McOstrich and Masha Tsiklauri of Insightful Corporation; Robert Page and Lois Snitkoff of Zope Corporation; Dr. Bill Pikounis of Merck Research Laboratories; Ron Roeber of the University of Nebraska; Winifred Shum of Verity; and Jim Smith of Johnson Controls. They have all improved the quality of this book through their efforts.

I would like to thank Jean Schauer, editor of *DM Review*, for use of content from my column, Enterprise Information Management, as well as from the feature article "Best Practices in Enterprise Information Portal Adoption: 5 Key Drivers," coauthored with Matt Aiken.

I must thank others who have helped from the beginning with this book. Matt Aiken, CEO of Redmont Corporation, recognized the need for this book and helped it reach fruition. Others have helped me understand both the business needs and technical issues behind information technology systems, including Roger Gough, Tom Leggette, and Dan Chrisman. Their insights have helped more than they know.

Thanks to Mary O'Brien, executive editor at Addison-Wesley Professional, for adding *Proven Portals* to the recognized ranks of Addison-Wesley books on information technology. I hope this book is judged by the company it keeps. I would like to thank Chrysta Meadowbrooke for her thorough and thoughtful copyediting. Thanks also to Brenda Mulligan, Alicia Carey, Elizabeth Ryan, and Tyrrell Albaugh of Addison-Wesley for their efforts to bring this book to market.

No one has helped more or deserves more credit for this book than my family. My children have encouraged me throughout the whole process, cheering on the chapter countdown like they were watching the New Year's Eve ball in Times Square. My wife, Kathy, a writer herself, knew what we were getting the family into when we took on this book, but she never had second thoughts. I could not have done it without her. Finally, I wish to thank my in-laws, Jane and Bill Aiken, who continue their two-decades-old habit of going out of their way to encourage and support every grand scheme Kathy and I come up with. They should know better by now.

# PART I

# Principles of Portal Design

# CHAPTER ONE

# Creating Frameworks for Organizing Information

Portal designers can learn much from architects and builders. Well-designed buildings are easy to use and structurally sound. We can find what we want, components like doors and windows appear in logical places, and, most importantly, the building stands up over time. We cannot go into a building and find the structural integrity the same way we can find the heating and ventilation units or the corner office. Structural integrity is a property of the way the building was designed and constructed; it is not a single feature added at some point in the construction process. The structural integrity of a portal is similar to that of a building. It is a fundamental property of the portal design, reflected in turn in visible characteristics, such as ease of use, functionality, and reliability.

In this chapter, we look into structural integrity from a user's perspective. The core question we address is "How will portal users find what they need?" Actually, we break this question into a number of more specific questions to which we can provide general but concrete answers.

First, we discuss how to organize information on a page. This may sound insignificant compared to other challenges that await us in portal development, but poorly designed pages hamper the portal's adoption. Next, we look at design patterns for logically grouping related content and applications to provide a sense of context for our users. We can all appreciate the sense of being in a particular section of a department store and knowing in general how to find other sections. We should provide something analogous for portal users. Without contexts users can easily become lost in an apparent jumble of hyperlinked pages. Finally, we look at specialized techniques (such as taxonomies, faceted content models, and visualization) that can aid navigation, especially in large and diverse portals. A case study shows how visualization and logical restructuring techniques improved customer care services for one organization.

Much has been written about usability and Web design techniques, and this book does not try to add to these well-discussed areas. The main concern here tends more toward architectural issues, which sometimes abut or even overlap with usability issues. For questions about usability and design layout, I defer to any of the well-written books on the subject such as *Don't Make Me Think* by Steve Krug and Roger Black [2000] and *Designing Web Usability* by Jakob Nielsen [1999]. I will address the types of structural elements required in well-designed portals but won't try to describe the finer details of their layout, formatting, and other visual elements.

## The Need for Structure in Portal Interface Design

When considering portal interface structure, it is useful to distinguish between the visible structures and the underlying structures. The visible structures provide the organization reflected in the designs of pages, groups of pages (known as subsites), and the entire portal itself. These structures are readily apparent to users.

The underlying structures are core services, such as authentication, access controls, and metadata management, as well as the policies and procedures that govern the evolution of the portal. These structures are not necessarily visible when they work well, but their absence is all too apparent. When users cannot work with essential applications because of access control problems or when navigation tools direct searchers to inappropriate content because of miscategorized metadata, users become all too aware of these underlying services.

### Page-Level Structures

Page-level structures include the distribution of content, applications, and navigation tools. Many pages use the basic three-panel structure shown in Figure 1.1. The top area contains global information about the site, the left side area contains navigation controls and links to commonly used objects, and the large central panel is home to the substantive content of the portal.

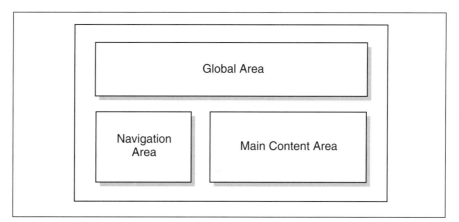

**Figure 1.1    Many portal pages use a basic three-part layout.**

The global area is consistent across the portal and often provides links to a home page, contact information, accessories, or other frequently used applications.

The navigation area provides a localized context for users. If you went to the human resources area of a portal you would expect to find navigation links to training, policies and procedures, benefits information, and related material; in a health and safety area of the portal you'd expect to find information on material safety, accident prevention, and reporting procedures. The role of the site navigation area is to provide an immediately visible and easily accessible path to related components in the portal while keeping the user from being overwhelmed by the full breadth of the portal.

There are several common approaches to organizing the navigation area. First, the area can be organized by subsite or neighborhood. The CNN Web site (http://www.cnn.com), for example, uses this approach by consistently listing subsites (such as Weather, Politics, Business, and Sports) in the navigation area. A variation on this model is to display subtopics when a topic is selected. A third approach focuses on tasks rather than content and is more appropriate for portals or subsites oriented toward content management. Yet another approach is a hybrid that combines content-oriented with task-oriented links. Care should be taken to clearly distinguish the two types of links, remembering that the purpose of the navigation section is to provide a sense of context. Intermixing content and task links could make it more difficult for users to perceive their location within the portal.

The main content area delivers the core information and application access that the users seek. By framing this information and the applications in navigational frameworks, you provide users immediate access to locally related topics as well as global landmarks, such as the portal home page.

### Grouping Pages: More Than One "Right" Way to Do It

An organizational model describes how entities are related. In the case of a portal, it describes how content, applications, and other resources are made accessible to users. The simplest model offers hyperlinking without restrictions. In this case, any page or resource can provide links to any others. This is the general model of the Web and the de facto organizational scheme for ungoverned intranets as well as the Internet. The advantage of this model is that decision making is completely decentralized so anyone can add content at any time to any part of the intranet. The disadvantage, so clear from the World Wide Web, is that this organizational scheme provides no point of reference for users. For example, if you find yourself at a page in such an intranet, there is no absolute reference point such as a home page or directory. All pages are equally important with regard to navigation, as depicted in Figure 1.2.

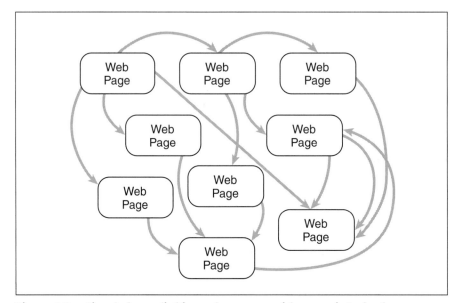

**Figure 1.2    Simple hyperlinking schemes provide no point of reference.**

Fortunately, most sites are no longer so freewheeling that we are left to navigate without some fixed references. Hierarchical organizational schemes provide an organizational structure with a top-level starting point and one or more levels of content. The simplest form of hierarchical organization is a tree with a root and links to lower-level pages. For practical purposes, most portals and Web sites also link across the hierarchy, as shown in Figure 1.3.

This type of nonhierarchical linking is required because simple hierarchies do not adequately model the way we think about information and how to find it. Consider a general topic such as "wireless phones." Where should this fit into a hierarchy? Some possibilities include:

1. Business > Services > Telecommunications > Mobile Services
2. Business > Office Products > Phone Systems > Wireless Phones
3. Consumer > Telecommunications > Wireless Phones

Each hierarchical categorization is reasonable; the most intuitive one depends on the context of the search. If the user is looking for a mobile phone service, the first categorization above appears logical; if he or she is interested in purchasing a wireless phone, the second makes the most sense; and if the user is looking for a wireless phone for home, the third categorization is the most likely

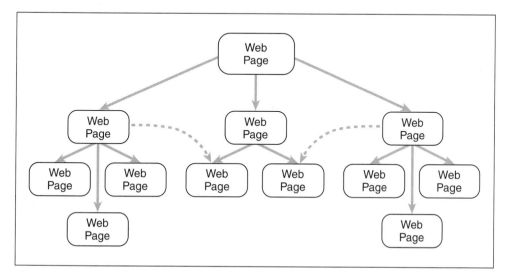

**Figure 1.3** Even hierarchical patterns need to cross-reference nodes to support the way users navigate a site.

to be followed. Clearly, a single hierarchical structure is not sufficient for even moderately complex portals. More importantly, there is no single correct answer about where to place a page in a hierarchy, so don't bother trying to find one.

### Organizing Multiple Ways with Facets

Instead, use a more flexible approach to navigating between pages. Multifaceted organizational schemes avoid the problem of hierarchies by accounting for the fact that an entity such as a product, application, or Web page can be classified along multiple dimensions. For example, let's assume a user is searching for a wireless phone, for less than $150, in silver or black with multiline support. Ideally, the user could navigate to information about phones, find wireless phones as a subcategory, shift to navigating by price, select the $125–$175 category, and finally narrow the search by color and functionality. In this example we have four facets: product category, cost, color, and feature set. When designing an information model, it is best to consider several facets or dimensions along which content is organized.

Metadata about categorization and content classification constitute facets or dimensions for organizing content. For example, a document published by the Health, Environment, and Safety Department on the proper disposal of chemical waste may be an official policy, published on a particular date, constituting compliance with a government regulation and broadly categorized as a safety document. The document type (policy), publication date, category (safety), and regulation status are all facets or attributes useful for organization and retrieval. One way to think about facets is as dimensions in a multidimensional space. Figure 1.4, for example, depicts the location of documents in a multidimensional space.

Facet-based information retrieval can help users target specific content more quickly than simple keyword searching or navigation through a directory. Facet-based searches should allow a combination of keyword searches and attribute searches, such as searching for all "policy" type documents that contain the phrase "toxic disposal" and were published between May 1, 2003, and July 1, 2003. This technique is especially powerful when working with product catalogs that list items described by several dimensions (e.g., cost, size, color, feature set).

Dimensions can use a list of values, a range of values, or hierarchical values and in this way is similar to many online analytic processing (OLAP) tools. Relational taxonomies can model hierarchical values, but continuous value attributes (e.g., cost, time) are best modeled with scalar variables such as strings, numbers, and Boolean values.

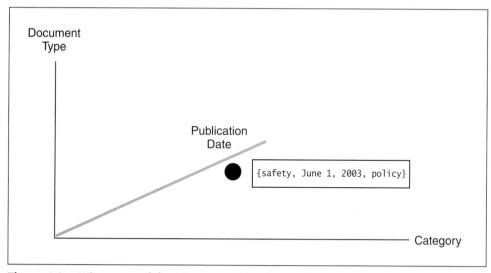

Document
Type

Publication
Date

{safety, June 1, 2003, policy}

Category

**Figure 1.4** **When organizing documents by facets, documents can be considered points in multidimensional space where each dimension is a facet.**

The dimensions should reflect the ways users describe or understand content since organizational structure, like a search tool, is a key method for facilitating information retrieval. A particularly large site, FirstGov (http://www.firstgov.gov), the official site of the U.S. government, uses multiple facets, including:

- Audience
- Topic
- Service
- Organization

The main page provides links to citizen, business, and government audience channels. The target pages of those links then list options by service. The service page in turn organizes content by topic. FirstGov's organizational model uses multiple facets and mixes those facets within paths from the home page to the content pages. This approach works well when you have information about usage patterns and frequently accessed pages. Analyzing log files from Web servers can provide key information about the most frequently accessed pages. By analyzing and grouping those pages, you can develop a rough categorization scheme based on facets.

Understanding how users think about the content and other resources in a portal is essential to developing a logical organizational model. Neither free-form links across a site nor rigid adherence to a hierarchical structure will serve the user community. Multifaceted organizational models provide the organizing structure of hierarchical systems and some of the flexibility of free-form linking within a controlled framework. Later in this chapter, we examine how complex facets can be organized using taxonomies.

### Flexible Organization with Navigation Sets and Other Design Patterns

Another approach to organizing links is to use a hybrid of the hierarchical and free-form hyperlinking approaches. With this technique, we make a decision that some dimension is more important than others, such as the organizational structure of a company or the categories of products. The hierarchy is based on this dimension. Within each branch of the hierarchy pages can be linked as needed to other pages in the same branch. The advantage of this approach is that it allows users to quickly find high-level topic areas (such as the human resources section of a company portal or the camping equipment offerings of an online store) while still allowing the site designer to customize links between related pages. These relatively closed-off areas of related pages are called **navigation sets**. Figure 1.5 shows this common navigation pattern.

A number of other patterns have evolved along with the development of the Web. These patterns provide a sense of well-defined location within a portal and

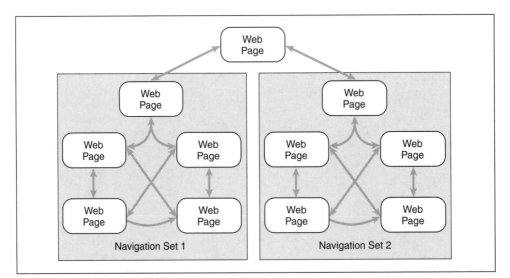

**Figure 1.5**   **Navigation sets are groups of highly linked pages with relatively few links outside the neighborhood. Exceptions include links to home pages, contact information, and other global content.**

provide rapid access to other well-defined places. Some of the most useful patterns (in addition to navigation sets) are listed below [Rossi et al.]. These patterns can be used independently but are often found together.

- *Landmarks:* Landmarks are links to entry points, large subsections of portals, or frequently used applications. CNN.com, for example, displays links to weather, politics, business, sports, and so on in the left side menu.
- *Nodes in context:* A variation on navigation sets are nodes in context. With this navigation pattern, the same content is repurposed for multiple uses. Depending on the use, the links associated with content vary. For example, an online retailer could list a new tent in both the camping equipment area and the new products area. In the former case, links from the tent display would lead to other camping equipment while the latter category would include links to other new products. Again, the point is to provide navigation links to logically related content to create a sense of context and intuitive navigation paths out of one navigation set and into another. Both navigation sets and nodes in context provide a fine-grained sense of context. Users also need a sense of context relative to the portal or site as a whole. That is the job of active references.
- *Active references:* Active references are indicators of one's position relative to the site as a whole or relative to a landmark. Directories such as Yahoo! and Google Directory use a list of nodes traversed in the directory. For example, see http://directory.google.com/Top/Computers/Internet/Web_Design_and_Development/, which uses an active link: Computers > Internet > Web Design and Development.

  Visual active references are excellent methods for depicting location within a larger context. This is especially applicable when content corresponds to a physical location, such as a room in a building or a street address. As the New York Metropolitan Museum of Art timeline of art history shows (http://www.metmuseum.org/toah/splash.htm), two or more contexts, in this case time and location, can be depicted simultaneously.
- *News:* Another common navigation pattern is the news section, which is used to prominently display important corporate information or new portal features. Many public news feeds are also available in XML formats, particularly the Rich Site Summary (RSS) scheme.

Together, these and other navigation patterns constitute an essential part of the overall information architecture of a portal. They provide a sense of context to the user and offer easily accessible links to significant or related sections of the portal. To ensure that the links are named logically and the user's experience is consistent across the portal, we must define labeling standards to identify the links that constitute these navigation patterns.

### Labeling: Pointing Users in the Right Direction

Labeling standards dictate how content, links, and other objects are named within a portal. At first blush, this may seem like a trivial consideration compared to others you have to deal with in a portal implementation. However, users constantly see and use the labeling system in a portal. Well-designed systems aid navigation and should be almost unnoticed by end users. Typically, when end users notice the labeling scheme it is because of a problem. The scheme may be inconsistent or ambiguous, or it may have some other aspect that puts an additional burden on the user to determine an appropriate action or understand the meaning of a link. The issues you must contend with include the following:

- Multiple terms that mean the same thing
- Terms with multiple meanings
- Controlled vocabularies

Not long after you begin work on labeling you realize there are many ways to describe an object. Choosing one term often pleases some users and leaves others disagreeing. Some objects, such as products, departments, and projects, have official names and so have an obvious label. Even in these cases, product names change over time and departments are reorganized; as a result, outdated terms can be found in older content. Nonetheless, standard terms should be used consistently throughout the portal. In many industries, controlled vocabularies or standard lists of terms have been developed by corporate librarians, information scientists, and others who have had to deal with information retrieval problems long before the advent of the Web. These industry standards can provide the basis for a labeling standard and minimize the time and effort required to develop your own.

When controlled vocabularies are not available, search log analysis can provide a starting point for labeling conventions. Search logs identify the terms used to query an intranet or portal and provide information about results as well. The frequency with which terms appear in the log can guide the selection of terms for the labeling standard.

Successful labeling schemes are built on two factors. First, the choice of labels should be based on either their use among the portal audience (as measured by search log analysis) or the terms used by other external sources (e.g., industry vocabularies). Second, the labels should be applied consistently through the portal. This also entails maintenance because labeling schemes change to reflect changes in the organization and general business environment.

## Organizing Content around Taxonomies

The organizational techniques just described provide the skeletal structure of well-designed portals. They provide a logical organization that spans individual pages up to the entire portal. It is now time to turn our attention to the fine-grained structures required to organize the content that surrounds the coarser-grained organizational structure. In this section we discuss taxonomies—a commonly used organizing framework—that organize information reflected in facets.

### Classifying Content with Taxonomies

Taxonomies are quickly gaining prominence as navigational tools in portals and with good reason. Taxonomies, or classification schemes, provide a high-level view of the content and other resources available in a portal. Search tools are useful when we are looking for a targeted piece of information, but taxonomies provide an easy-to-use browsing method. Users do not have to know what terms to search for or even whether specific information exists. Taxonomies allow us to move quickly from high-level groupings (e.g., Business, Weather, Politics, and Sports) to narrow subjects (e.g., Marketing, Finance, Investment, and so on).

While it is often easy to start constructing taxonomies, the process becomes more difficult as you move to more specific categories and realize there may be multiple ways to classify the same topic. This leads to the first rule of taxonomy development: There is not a single correct taxonomy. There are many. For example, suppose you want to find a speech by the president of the Federal Reserve Bank of Chicago using the Yahoo! directory (http://www.yahoo.com). You could find the bank's Web site in at least two different ways using the directory. One way is to start at Home and then follow the taxonomy based on organizational structure :

> **Home > Government > U.S. Government > Agencies > Independent > Federal Reserve System > Federal Reserve Banks**

Alternatively, you could follow the taxonomy based on geographical organization:

> **Home > Regional > U.S. States > Illinois > Cities > Chicago > Community > Government > Federal Reserve Bank of Chicago**

What seems like a logical organization is a function of how we think about a topic, not how the topic is organized according to a predefined scheme. We are not under the same constraints as librarians who have to manage physical assets. A book can be in only one location at a time, so librarians need to adopt a single arbitrary scheme (such as the Library of Congress Subject Headings or the Dewey Decimal System) to effectively manage these assets. Digital assets are easily categorized with multiple schemes. However, with this flexibility comes a new problem: integrating these multiple schemes.

For those developers convinced that a taxonomy is needed for their portals, the next question is where to begin.

## Building Taxonomies

Portal developers have a number of options for building taxonomies.

- Start with an existing third-party taxonomy.
- Use enterprise structures (e.g., directory structures).
- Use automated clustering.

Each has its benefits and drawbacks, but using a combination of these techniques can often meet most needs.

The quickest way to develop a taxonomy is to simply use an existing one. Publicly available classification schemes, such as the Library of Congress Subject Headings, cover a wide range of topics but may not be suited to commercial organizations because of their focus on comprehensive coverage of top-level topics. Industry- and discipline-specific taxonomies are widely available and often provide a good starting point. Remember to match the coverage of the taxonomy to your specific needs. For example, a taxonomy from an electrical engineering organization will work well for electrical engineers but may not work as well for teams that combine electrical engineering, computer science, and chemistry experts. Multidisciplinary teams tend to focus on particular problems (e.g., low power consumption circuit design), and taxonomies organized around those problems are better suited than discipline-centric ones. General business taxonomies are available from news aggregation services that have often developed the classification schemes for their own use. Even if a third-party taxonomy is not a perfect fit "out of the box," it can be combined with schemes developed in-house.

For as long as we have had subdirectories in file systems, we have been categorically organizing content. Many organizations have large shared directories organized around business processes, organizational structures, and ad hoc practices. These directory structures are useful starting points for building taxonomies because they tend to reflect the way users, at least some users, organize their work. When using network directory structures as a guide we need to remember that some subdirectories are created for ad hoc tasks, some are used simply to share files much like an ftp site, and some are no longer used but continue to exist because of poor directory management practices. Nonetheless, within the sometimes sprawling directory structures we can find elements of organizational structures that reflect existing business processes.

Automatic clustering of documents can also provide insight into the logical grouping of content. Basically, the process involves analyzing patterns within documents and grouping documents with similar patterns. This technique is useful when the logical grouping of documents is not clear, for example, when doing research in an unfamiliar domain. Clustering can definitely help discern the groups of documents, but it cannot be the sole technique used to define taxonomies. Not all groups identified by the clustering tool will make sense. Clustering tools can name the groups using terms that frequently occur in the member documents, but these are generally insufficient labels for end users.

When developing taxonomies, our primary focus must be on the way users think about their domain, not what third-party experts have decreed and not on the output of automatic categorization algorithms. There is no "right" answer. The best taxonomies are the ones that match the users' model of the organization and its processes.

Taxonomies are typically, although not exclusively, hierarchical. Taxonomies allow us to think about topics in relation to broader and narrower topics. When we make these distinctions between broader and narrower topics we are doing it based on some overriding concept. For example, when we navigate from a point labeled "United States" to "Illinois" to "Chicago," the overriding concept is geography. When we navigate from "United States" to "Federal Government" to "Supreme Court," the overriding concept is government structure. Clearly we can categorize topics in different ways depending on our particular interest at the time.[1]

---

[1] For readers especially interested in keeping up-to-date on developments in taxonomies and other information organization schemes, I suggest subscribing to Ramana Roa's *Information Flow* newsletter (http://www.ramanarao.com/informationflow/).

Similar structures exist in OLAP applications. We can think about sales figures by product, by sales region, and by time. Traditionally, these organizing principles are called **dimensions**. In the world of taxonomies and content management, we refer to these as **facets**.

## Visualization Tools for Portal Organization

Structural organization techniques like taxonomies, facets, and metadata can aid information retrieval, but even with well-designed search queries that target particular subsets of content, a user can still be overwhelmed with the number of items returned by conventional search engines. Visualization tools effectively reduce information overload by mapping content to visual representations that aggregate content while highlighting significant relationships. For example, visualization tools can rapidly show a high-level structure, such as a site map, while allowing users to easily navigate to a particular area for more detail. In addition, these schemes depict content areas that users may not know exist and shows a broad context for content.

A number of different techniques are used to visualize content repositories such as portals. One technique, called **focus+context**, highlights one area (the focus) while showing the relationship of that area to other areas (the context). InXight's VizServer uses focus+context to allow users to navigate hyperlinked documents. A study at Xerox Palo Alto Research Center (PARC), which spun off InXight to commercialize the visualization tools, found that users could browse 62% faster with a focus+context tool than with a traditional two-dimensional tree layout such as Microsoft Explorer [Pirolli et al.].

Relational navigation is a visualization technique that depicts database relationships rather than hyperlinks and is useful for browsing database-driven sites. ThinkMap from Plumb Design software is just one example of this type of tool.

Portals frequently integrate content from hyperlink sources, databases, file systems, and other repositories. In those cases, visualization constructs based on business processes and structures tend to work best. The case study on Center Partners describes one such application.

**CASE STUDY:** Visualization and Logical Restructuring Improve Customer
                   Care Services at Center Partners

The outsourced customer care industry is demanding on all parties involved. Customer care center providers have to understand the details of their clients' business policies, products, and services and convey that understanding to callers with widely varying needs. Client companies entrust customer care centers to attract new customers, build customer loyalty, provide technical support, and provide other critical points of contact with their customers. Maintaining quality standards is essential. The agents who operate the centers are under the sometimes conflicting demands of maintaining quality service while minimizing the average call time. Training agents and providing them with rapid information retrieval tools is essential to the success of these operations. One customer care center, Center Partners (http://*www.centerpartners.com*), used enterprise portal and visualization-based information retrieval software to improve quality measures while reducing call time to the point of generating an additional $500,000 per year in revenue.

**The Problem: Poorly Organized Distributed Content**

Center Partners operates seven offices with 2,500 customer care agents throughout the United States to serve Fortune 500 clients. This customer care firm generates annual revenue of $100 million and serves customers in industries ranging from insurance and financial services to pharmaceuticals and high tech. This service provider, like many in this area, measures operational success by the time required to handle customer calls and the level of service quality provided. Reducing the average call-handling time increases the efficiency of the center; quality measures are required by contractual agreements with customers. Both objective measures are served by improving agents' access to information.

The breadth and depth alone of the information customer care agents must tap in the course of their work demands a structured content management mechanism. Unfortunately, Center Partners does not control its information sources; the clients do. It is not unusual for the firm to depend on corporate extranets designed for multiple purposes that lack the features needed for fast-paced call center operations. David Geiger, Chief Information Officer of Center Partners, reported one client changed 2,800 extranet pages in a single month. "The dynamic nature of the content made it nearly impossible for a busy agent to be up-to-date on the latest information. Moreover, the site, as is common with most Web sites, was difficult to navigate and did not offer any useful search capabilities" [TheBrain Technologies 2002]. Even well-designed customer sites are more likely suited for online shopping than the kind of troubleshooting tasks faced by agents.

Since Center Partners could not redesign its customers' sites, the company instead deployed a middle-tier content organization application in its portal that allowed them to organize content in a manner that better fits the way the agents work. Figure 1.6 shows how a middle tier hides the underlying complexity of the application.

### The Solution: Visualization and Logical Restructuring

Center Partners chose BrainEKP from TheBrain Technologies Corporation (http://www.thebrain.com), an enterprise knowledge portal tool with strong visualization and search features, to provide a middle layer for the new navigation scheme without redesigning customer content. BrainEKP

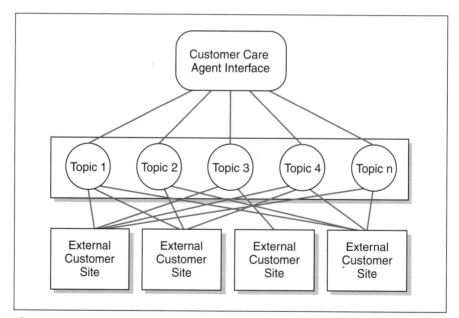

Figure 1.6     A middle tier can provide a logical organization that reflects users' understanding of a domain without requiring changes to the underlying implementation.

completely resides on Center Partners servers; it is external to customer sites and requires no changes on the customers' part. Domain experts at Center Partners first organized content into topics that support particular tasks, such as describing a refund policy or troubleshooting a service problem. Each topic (called a *thought* in TheBrain's terminology) provides links to content distributed across the Web, intranets, file systems, and databases.

Unlike typical search engines, selecting a topic in BrainEKP immediately displays related topics as well as content specific to the topic of interest. For example, navigating to the Repair topic displays the Tier 1 Repair Website while depicting links to vendor-specific repair information, as shown in Figure 1.7. BrainEKP also provides full-featured search using an embedded version of Convera RetrievalWare. To further improve the effectiveness of BrainEKP, Center Partners allows agents to customize their information sources and add their own notes and links.

The return on investment was clear for Center Partners. Quality increased enough to generate an expected additional $500,000 in revenue

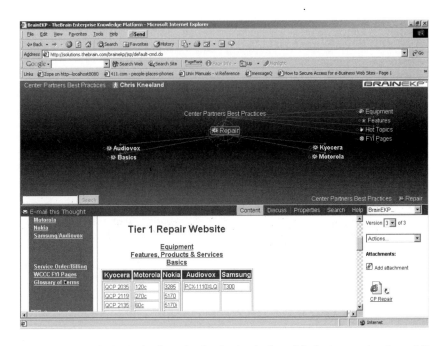

**Figure 1.7**    BrainEKP depicts the logical relationship between topics while displaying detailed content on the topic of focus.

over the course of a year and dropped the average call-handling time by 43 seconds.

**Best Practices**

Center Partners realized these gains by recognizing a number of best practices, including the following:

- **Use visualization to reduce the time required to retrieve information.**
- **Customize the logical organization of content through a middle tier rather than implementing a single organizational scheme that serves all usage models.**
- **Allow users to customize the portal to meet their particular needs and style.**

Content used with permission of Harlan Hugh, chief technology officer and co-founder of TheBrain; David Gerger, CIO Call Center Partners, Chris Kneeland, chief learning officer, Call Center Partners, TheBrain Technologies Corporation.

## Emerging Trends and Technologies

As the scope of enterprise portals grows, the associated information retrieval problems will worsen if new technologies and techniques are not enlisted. One of the primary values of portals is that they allow us rapid access to a broad range of content and applications; however, that benefit is undermined by the very success and growth of portals. To ensure that we can keep ahead of the information overload problem today we must design portals with effective search, directory, and information architectures. In the near future we will require additional tools to manage content and to allow our applications to assume more responsibility for weeding out irrelevant information.

Researchers have worked on problems in natural language processing and knowledge representation for over 40 years, and the practical, commercial benefit of those undertakings will be realized in enterprise information portals (among other applications). The most pressing problem for advanced portal users and designers is to create applications customized to particular users' needs. Several systems and technologies are especially important to this effort.

- *Cyc:* Cyc is a knowledge base of over 100,000 terms, over 1,000,000 facts or assertions, and a reasoning engine for drawing conclusions about those facts. Cyc was developed by Cycorp (http://www.cyc.com) and has been used in organizations ranging from Lycos, which uses it to improve search engine results, to the U.S. Department of Defense, which has invested heavily in Cyc development for military applications. The use of large-scale, general knowledge bases may help improve search and navigation in portals by improving the modeling of user behavior.

- *MESH:* Medical Subject Headings (MESH) is a controlled vocabulary thesaurus developed by the U.S. National Library of Medicine with over 21,000 descriptors, over 132,000 supplementary descriptors in a separate chemical thesaurus, and thousands of cross-references between terms. MESH is used to index articles from over 4,000 biomedical journals as well as the MEDLINE database.
- *WordNet:* WordNet is an online lexical reference developed by researchers at Princeton University based on psycholinguistic theories about human memory. WordNet contains over 146,000 words and over 195,000 word senses. WordNet contains both word senses (e.g., ten meanings of the word *book* and five meanings of *search*) and synonym sets of related terms. This lexical resource is currently used in some search engines to improve search results.

Cyc, MESH, and WordNet are currently used or have the potential for use in enterprise portals. These are just three examples of the general and specialized knowledge representation tools that are of growing importance to portals. Much of the work now under way in knowledge representation centers around three approaches.

1. Ontologies are organized representations of concepts, often for specific domains, such as pharmaceuticals, health care, and electronics. The Cyc knowledge base supports multiple ontologies. (See http://ksl-web.stanford .edu/kst/ontology-sources.html.)
2. Topic maps are groups of addressable information objects (e.g., documents) around topics and the relationship between those objects. The TopicsMaps .org consortium is developing standards to use XML to develop topic maps for the Web. (See http://www.topicmaps.org/.)
3. Semantic Web is an effort to embody semantic information in Web resources so that both humans and automated agents can more effectively manage those resources. (See http://www.w3.org/2001/sw/.)

With these technologies emerging in the portal arena, what can users realistically expect in the next few years? First, anticipate improved search capabilities in highly specialized domains like pharmaceuticals and medicine. Second, expect incremental improvements in general search and categorization. Third, do not expect radical breakthroughs. Technologies like the semantic Web hold great promise, but much of the work is still in the research phase. Finally, we will continue to have significant amounts of manual work, from developing and tuning ontologies to defining topic maps. These technologies, however, will make it easier to share knowledge bases across applications.

## Conclusion

Sound structural design is as important to portals as it is to buildings. The interface is a user's introduction to the portal. It is also the key to accessing the content and services provided by the portal. As we design and deploy portals we should consider how to organize information and applications in a way that makes sense to users. This of course is a problem for several reasons. First, there are many users and their needs vary. Second, how even a single user uses the portal depends on the task he or she is trying to accomplish. If performing a routine task, for example, entering a time card, the user will want rapid access to the application. This is no place for needless clicks through a hierarchical set of applications. On the other hand, if the user is researching a new product line, he or she will want to browse through related content, follow promising paths of related information, and quickly narrow the search in response to hunches about new angles on the problem. The only way to meet these needs is to provide multiple ways to navigate and to keep the overall organization consistent.

Content within pages should follow a pattern. The three-panel model balances formal structure with flexible organization of content. Landmarks, active links, and other navigation techniques will help users quickly move around within the portal.

Organizing content around navigation sets provides a sense of context for users. They will be able to move easily between related pages while the page-level navigation patterns, like landmarks back to a home page, will help the user move to other areas quickly.

As the amount of information in the portal grows, users will need additional support to find what they need. Taxonomies and faceted models provide users with tools to see the forest and quickly focus on a specific tree. For especially large portals, visualization techniques can further improve navigation.

With a grounding in techniques for designing interfaces, in the next chapter we will turn our attention to the underlying frameworks that support the portal's core functions and services.

## References

Krug, Steve, and Roger Black. 2000. *Don't Make Me Think: A Common Sense Approach to Web Usability.* Indianapolis, IN: Que.

Nielsen, Jakob. 1999. *Designing Web Usability: The Practice of Simplicity.* Indianapolis, IN: New Riders.

Pirolli, Peter, Stuart K. Card, and Mija M. Van der Wege. (Year not stated.) "The Effect of Information Scent on Searching Information Visualization of Large Tree Structures." Accessed in June 2003 at *http://www.inxight.com/pdfs/PARCstudy.pdf.*

Rossi, Gustov, Daniel Schwabe, and Fernando Lyardet. (Year not stated.) "Improving Web Information Systems with Navigational Patterns." Accessed in June 2003 at *http://www8.org/w8-papers/5b-hypertext-media/improving/improving.html.*

TheBrain Technologies. 2002. "Center Partners: Improving Call Handle Times and Agent Best Practices." Received via e-mail from TheBrain.

# CHAPTER TWO

# Using a Three-Tier Architecture

In this chapter we will delve into the logical architecture that underlies successful portal implementations. Although vendors and designers have a variety of ways to implement portal applications, most center on a basic three-tier architecture: the presentation layer, the application layer, and the information services layer (Figure 2.1). The philosophy behind this breakdown is to separate the major activities of portal applications into logical sections for display, processing logic, and data services. Displays are managed by the presentation tier, processing logic by the application tier, and data services by the enterprise information systems (EIS) tier.

This chapter examines each tier, including the role it plays, the services it provides, and the interactions it has with the other layers. Of course, in reality, portal architecture involves more than just plugging three components together so we also look into the internal structure of each layer to better understand the implications of the design choices we make. First we examine the structure of the presentation layer, which is responsible for providing the user interface.

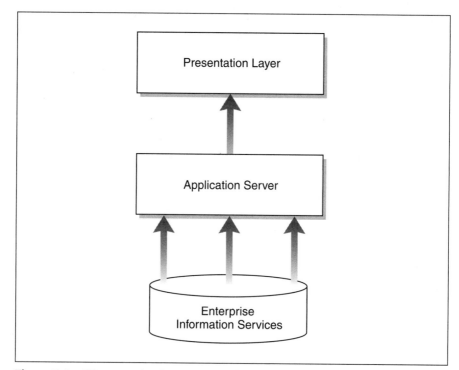

**Figure 2.1    The most basic portal architecture consists of presentation, application, and information services layers.**

## Tier 1: The Presentation Layer

The role of the presentation layer is to provide a unified view to segmented business processes. Before portals, users were accustomed to working with a variety of desktop applications, such as word processors, spreadsheets, and presentation programs. Over time, these common applications became more integrated and at least had a common look and feel. While that move was a step in the right direction, users were too often switching between several distinct programs to keep up with their daily work. For example, it is not unusual for a single user to:

- Start a terminal emulation program to access a mainframe for financial information
- Log on to a UNIX server through a TELNET session to get daily production information

- Phone someone in another department to get information from a report that the user cannot generate because her or his PC does not have the necessary software installed
- Use e-mail to share documents with project team members

The problems with this scenario are obvious. Too much time is spent moving between applications, frustrating users and creating inefficiencies. Enterprise- and department-level applications all require usernames and passwords, and users inadvertently create potential security problems by reusing passwords, keeping written password lists, and remaining logged into applications they might need later in the day. To eliminate these problems, we need a combination of a single interface to multiple applications and a system to manage each user's security credentials and provide access to systems on an as-needed basis. The presentation layer provides the basis for a unified interface as well as the hooks to integrate with a single sign-on process.

### Interface Design for Portals

One of the key advantages of portals is that they allow us to integrate a wide range of applications for a number of different audiences, including those listed below:

- Customers
- Employees
- Supply chain partners
- Executive decision makers
- The general public

Even with the diverse needs of these audiences, a small number of common design elements can meet most needs. Figure 2.2 shows a typical portal layout for a consumer portal, and Figure 2.3 provides an example of a business intelligence portal for internal use.

In the business-to-consumer realm, portal interfaces typically include several elements:

- A banner emphasizing products or service branding
- A hierarchical menu of products and services
- The ability to log in for personalized information
- Main information and promotions

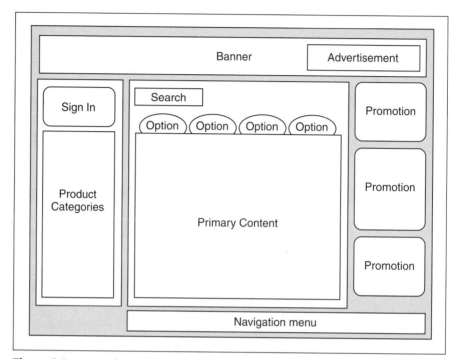

**Figure 2.2    A business-to-consumer portal must make information and
services readily accessible.**

These elements generally offer a mix of static information, like the banner,
and dynamically generated content, such as promotions. From the presentation
layer perspective, how the content is generated is irrelevant (that is for the middle
tier to address); what *is* important is how the information should be rendered for
the user.

### Interface Design Components

Enterprise information portals (EIPs) are more varied than e-commerce sites but
still have common characteristics. First, access to information is customized so
logging into the portal is the first step. Once the user is authenticated, the presentation layer provides dynamically generated content such as the following:

- Links to static HTML reports
- Links to business intelligence tools for ad hoc querying and analysis
- Third-party news feeds for industry-specific information

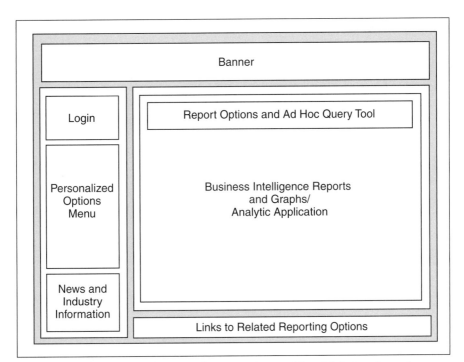

**Figure 2.3** **Enterprise information portals provide a high-level road map to a variety of performance indicators.**

- Content management features for publishing and sharing documents
- Access to collaboration tools such as threaded discussion groups

In both portal examples above, the interface is composed of a series of items framed in distinct regions. The complexity of items ranges from simple objects (e.g., URLs and images) to applets (e.g., calendars and calculators) to component-based applications (e.g., query and visualization tools).

Regardless of the template used for organizing information, designers need to determine how content will be rendered in the browser. The common methods are:

- HTML
- Plug-ins
- Downloaded applets

Each has its advantages and usually involves a trade-off between simplicity and functionality.

*The Tried and True: HTML*

HTML is the easiest way to render content in a browser. Publishing tools automate much of the basic coding. The markup language's simplicity is also its greatest weakness, and a number of techniques have been created to extend the functionality of HTML. The first extension helps separate data from formatting and the second adds more flow of control options.

Maintaining a consistent look and feel across a Web site or portal application can become unmanageable with basic HTML, but two techniques can help. The first, Cascading Style Sheets (CSS), defines rules for how a browser should display a particular type of HTML object. For example, a style sheet could define the color and font size for heading tags (e.g., <H1> and <H2>). Any HTML document linked to that style sheet would then display headings according to the defined style. CSS is especially useful when large numbers of relatively static HTML pages maintain a standard look and feel. When a broad range of dynamic information is displayed by Web applications, XML and XSL Transformations is the preferred option. Like CSS, XSL Transformations are formatting rules but they also support methods for mapping XML data into HTML. The advantage of XML and XSL is that they promote the separation of responsibilities we want in a portal architecture. When a server in the middle-tier application layer returns data to the presentation layer, it can generate a stream of XML data and leave the transformations and formatting to another component. The XSL Transformations, defined elsewhere in the application, can create HTML code to display the results in a browser or format the data for other types of devices, such as wireless personal digital assistants (PDAs) or cell phones.

Scripting languages such as JavaScript, ASP, and PHP allow for more control over how content is rendered than is available in HTML. Developers generally keep complex logic encapsulated in server-side components, like JavaBeans, to prevent HTML documents (whether static or generated) from becoming unwieldy. This also follows the general philosophy of the three-tier architecture, which is that each layer has particular responsibilities and that, to maximize flexibility and maintainability, the responsibilities should not be mixed. The HTML code sent from the server to the browser should have minimal control logic.

One exception to this rule is for data validation. Rather than burdening the middle-tier servers with simple data validation ("Is that start date earlier than the end date?"), the client platform should handle it. This also saves network traffic, which means a faster response to the user and also leaves the servers to address more complex validation ("Does this customer have sufficient credit to validate this order?").

HTML, even with scripting languages, cannot create the same type of interfaces many users have become accustomed to in client/server environments. In that case, a plug-in or downloaded component is required.

### Extending Browser Functionality: Plug-Ins

Unlike HTML and scripting languages, which are downloaded to browsers as Web pages are invoked, plug-ins are additional browser components installed on the client machine along with the browser application. Plug-ins are persistent so they need to be downloaded and installed only once. These components extend browser capabilities to meet specific needs, such as supporting streaming video and audio, displaying particular file types, and providing instant messaging. Plug-ins provide specific nonstandard features for browsers that are used across applications. When the complexity of the required interface moves beyond scripting and plug-ins, then applets are used.

### Applications in the Browser: Applets

Applets are Java programs designed to execute on a client using the browser's Java Virtual Machine (JVM). The advantage of this approach is that a developer can create a custom application in Java that is downloaded as needed; it is not necessary to install executables on a client machine. The major drawback from a user perspective is that additional time is required to download the applet. This may not be as much of an issue on corporate networks with Ethernet speeds if the applet is not downloaded too frequently, but the bandwidth needed for rapid downloads is not available to many consumer Internet users.

The combination of HTML (along with its formatting and scripting extensions), plug-ins, and applets provides the foundation for building flexible user interfaces in a browser-based environment. Managing multiple applications within the same browser is the responsibility of both the presentation tier and the application server tier. This shared task is managed through portlets.

## Portlets: The Bridge to the Middle Tier

Web page designers have free reign to determine how they use HTML, plug-ins, and applets in a Web site. When working in an integrated portal environment however, developers do not have the full freedom and flexibility available when working with simple Web pages.

Portal servers, which reside in the middle tier, provide the basic operating environment for generating content rendered through the portal. To ensure a consistent and reliable framework for combining arbitrary elements in a unified portal application, each component application (a **portlet** or **gadget** as they are sometimes called) needs to follow certain rules and conventions. In many ways, the portal server is analogous to the operating system in a client/server environment—it provides some services and prescribes how processes will interact with other processes. Portal servers provide basic services, such as user authentication, access controls, and application management (that is, portlet management); more specialized features, such as advanced search capabilities, news streams, hierarchical menus, reporting and graphing, and customized services, are delivered through custom applications or portlets. Figure 2.4 shows how portlets fit into the three-tier architecture.

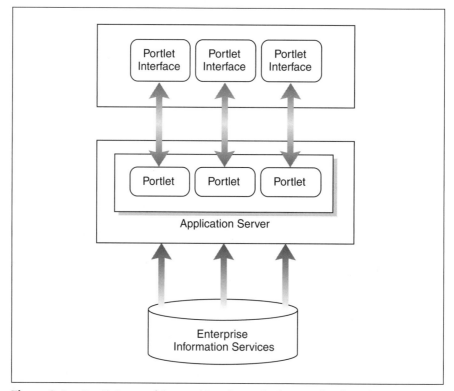

**Figure 2.4    Portlets provide services through the application tier and interface with the user at the presentation tier.**

Portal servers such as IBM WebSphere Portal, Oracle Portal, and Plumtree Corporate Portal all support portlets. All major portal servers provide basic portlets, and other software vendors often create portlets to access their applications from popular portal platforms. Portal application developers can also create their own portlets for custom requirements.

Frequently portlets are written in Java, but other commonly used Web languages (e.g., Perl) are also supported, and in some cases proprietary languages (e.g., Oracle's PL/SQL) can be used as well. In some cases, portal servers use a language-specific application programming interface (API) that makes it difficult to implement portlet services in other languages. The advent of Web services has changed that. Web services allow consumer and provider processes to communicate with XML-structured messages and the Simple Object Access Protocol (SOAP) over HTTP. With Web services, a component can be developed in any language and executed on any platform that uses these standards.

As we shall see in the next section, the heart of the framework is in the middle tier, the application server.

## Tier 2: The Application Server Layer

In many ways the application server tier is the brains of the portal. It is here that much of the work gets done. Server-side processing of servlets occurs here, business rules are executed here, data from multiple data sources is integrated here, and the core of portal utilities (e.g., search and navigation) resides here. Of course, this tier also controls access to data sources.

Before going much further, it is time for a few caveats. First, for the rest of the discussion we will refer to a single application server in a portal application. In reality, there could be multiple servers acting in concert to provide load balancing and failover protection.

Second, there could be multiple layers of application servers. For example, a search engine running on one server could act as part of a federated search system that makes search requests to another search engine. In other cases, a Web service on one server could make calls to other Web services running on a business partner's server. An e-commerce server might request a credit check of a customer from a third-party service, then query a supplier service about a drop shipment in another step, and then confirm and book an order with an internal order fulfillment system. We will ignore this level of detail here. Our goal is not to delve into the intricacies of designing distributed systems but to simply provide a common reference model for understanding the basic building blocks of portals. (If you're interested in those intricacies, see Britton [2001] for a start.)

Third, not all the work actually occurs in the application server. The simplified model used here assumes that the EIS tier is a passive repository that only responds to requests for information from the application server. That is not how it always works. Sometimes portlets directly access data sources without going through the application server. More often than not, data sources are actually complex transaction processing systems, like enterprise resource planning systems (ERP systems) or customer relationship management systems (CRM systems). For our purposes, though, we can ignore the inner workings of these systems. We will simply treat them as logical data sources that respond to data manipulation requests.

Now back to our simplified model and description of the basic services the middle tier provides. The middle tier houses much of the core processing in Web-based applications. The presentation tier provides input to the application server as well as manages the display of this tier's output. The EIS tier provides much of the grist for the application server mill. This leaves quite a bit for the application server to manage, including the following:

- Integration of data from multiple sources
- Application of business rules
- Content management
- Collaboration
- Adaptive content services
- Search and categorization
- Security and user administration

Some of these services, such as security and user administration, are common to almost all Web-based applications. Others, for example, search and categorization, are relevant to only particular types of applications. The one common element of all these services is that the bulk of their functions occur in the application server.

### Integration of Data from Multiple Sources

Portals are frequently used to provide integrated, single-point access to an organization's varied information systems. Figure 2.5 shows an example of a portal that provides access to documents, business intelligence information, news, and collaboration tools. Each of these applications runs in through a separate portlet

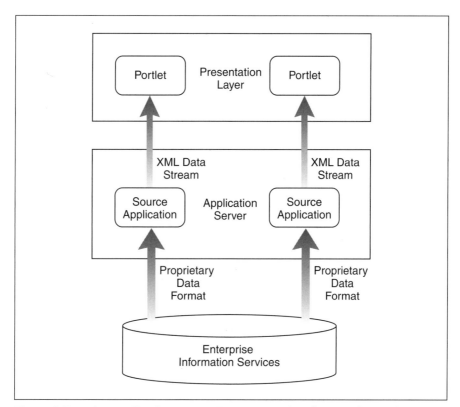

**Figure 2.5    The application server layer maps data in proprietary formats into standard XML formats so portlets do not need to adapt to the idiosyncrasies of legacy applications.**

and operates independently of the others. This is an example of presentation-layer, or shallow, integration.

The most significant advantage of this type of integration is that it is relatively simple to accomplish. Most portal tools have easy-to-use configuration managers that allow portal administrators and users to rapidly customize the look and feel of a portal and add or remove portlets.

The main disadvantage of this approach is that it does not exploit the inherent links between business processes and their related applications. For example, a business intelligence report might display information about insurance claims for a customer but might not link to the customer's policy, claims records, and authorizations. This deeper level of integration must occur at the application server or prior to that in the data provider applications.

Business processes, such as order processing, depend on the integration of multiple applications for taking orders, checking credit status, fulfilling orders, and invoicing for those orders. Programs running in the application server can bridge these systems by managing the workflow between them and ensuring that the data produced by one system is properly formatted and streamed to the next application in the overall process (Figure 2.6).

Application servers provide many of the messaging and transaction processing services required to ensure that these business processes are treated as atomic units. By creating atomic processes, the application server can prevent incomplete transactions, such as shipping an order without also ensuring an invoice has been created for it.

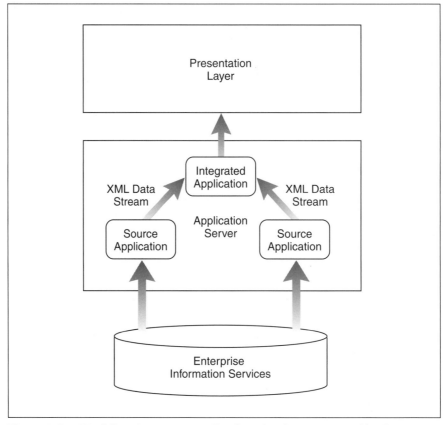

**Figure 2.6    Workflow between applications is often managed in the application server layer.**

### Application of Business Rules

Business rules are directives, policies, and procedures that dictate how business is done within an organization. Many industries, like insurance, health care, and financial services, need to support large numbers of business rules that cross application boundaries. Rather than maintain business rules in a number of different applications, many system designers separate the rules from the execution model of an application and use a rule processing engine that serves multiple applications.

### Content Management

Application servers often provide content management services to orchestrate the display and maintenance of text, images, audio, and video for dynamic Web sites and across the organization. These services include access controls on publishing and viewing, workflow, and integration with e-commerce applications.

### Collaboration

Collaboration services are frequently part of EIPs and knowledge management applications and include such services as:

- E-mail
- Threaded discussions
- Instant messaging
- Expert database
- Video conferencing

Most of these services could exist easily outside of the portal, but the value proposition of integrating them in the application server is that users have a single point of access, but more importantly, their integration improves the usefulness of individual tools. For example, a user might require help determining the eligibility of a health insurance customer to claim coverage for a particular medical procedure. Searching an expert database with a few keywords provides links to a number of individuals and their profiles as well as links to discussion threads containing their postings. After reviewing several topics, the user identifies an expert who is likely to have the needed answer and starts an instant messaging dialog.

### Adaptive Content Services

Adaptive content services change the content provided to a user based on the needs and interests of the user. There are three basic types of adaptive content services:

1. Customization
2. Collaborative filtering
3. Personalization

All three methods require database support. Customization uses direct user feedback, for example, from an online questionnaire, to create an interest profile. This technique is often used to select areas of interest from a news provider. Collaborative filtering and automated personalization use separate processes to identify content and product for users.

Collaborative filtering techniques analyze the viewing or buying patterns of an individual to identify another customer, sometimes called a **mentor**, who appears to have similar interests. This mentor's past behavior is used as a guide to find content or products that would be of interest to the individual. If a mentor bought Product X, it is assumed that customers associated with that mentor are likely to buy Product X.

Automated personalization uses a range of data mining techniques to group or cluster similar types of customers and identifies products with a high likelihood of cross-selling. This technique is computationally the most difficult.

### Search and Categorization

As the quantity of information increases, so does the need for search and categorization tools. Portal search engines are sometimes limited to indexing just the content stored within the portal, but increasingly enterprise search vendors are extending the reach of their tools to include documents and other text sources in file systems, document management systems, e-mail folders, and database applications.

Crawling and harvesting are two approaches to search. Crawling methods use processes to retrieve content from a variety of sources and build a single, centralized index. Most Web search engines use this model. Harvesting, or federated search, works with a number of search engines that each index a portion of the total content accessible to end users. When a federated search engine receives a query, it passes the request to other search engines, compiles the results, and displays a single result set to the user. Harvesting approaches are especially useful in portal applications when existing applications, such as document management systems, already manage index content for their own search purposes. Figure 2.7 depicts the difference between crawling-based and harvest-based search models.

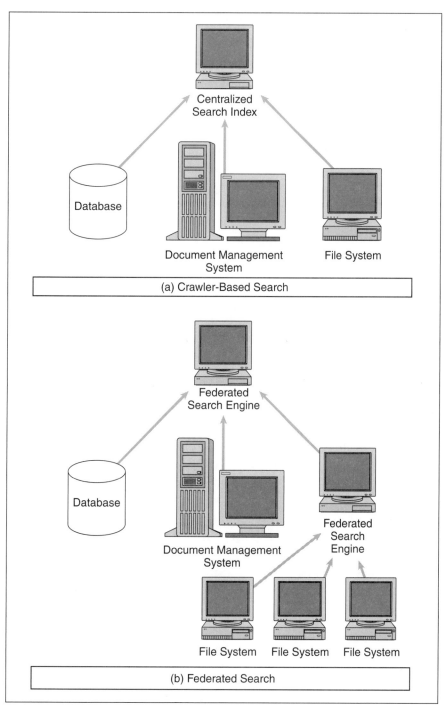

Centralized
Search Index

Database

Document Management
System

File System

(a) Crawler-Based Search

Federated
Search Engine

Database

Document Management
System

Federated
Search
Engine

File System    File System    File System

(b) Federated Search

**Figure 2.7    Crawling methods (a) use a single index while harvesters
(b) share the work among several search engines.**

As the scope and extent of enterprise contents grows, the relevancy of search results becomes more difficult to manage. Even though a search query might find a large number of matches, too often these are not actually related to the topic the user is researching. On the other hand, the search can easily miss documents that are relevant to the user's interests but do not contain the specific keywords or phrase specified in the query. These two problems, called **poor precision** and **poor recall**, respectively, have plagued information retrieval systems since their inception. A number of alternative search and indexing techniques can improve performance, including categorizing content into topical areas relevant to an organization.

One of the top business requirements for EIPs is to bring some level of organization to enterprise content, and categorization is the first step to imposing order on the seeming chaos. The process starts by specifying relevant categories and then defines business rules or trains a statistical classification tool to actually perform the categorization. Frequently categories are arranged into hierarchical schemes called **taxonomies**. Managing these categories and taxonomies and then integrating them with search services are commonly required services for portals.

### Security and User Administration

Security comes in several forms within a portal. The portal itself controls access to content, portlets, and customization features. These features are controlled with conventional users, groups, and access control lists within the portal engine. When the user needs to interact with another application, for example, to retrieve a record from a database, the user needs to log in or authenticate against the data source. Single sign-on services minimize the need for users to log in to individual applications by managing the process for them.

The application server tier covers a broad range of services. Most of the work of managing the portal occurs in this layer. A common framework is essential in this layer to ensure that developers can deploy enterprise components in the application server and have them function along with services. Fortunately this need was recognized early in the development of portals, and portal vendors have developed their products with these frameworks in mind.

## Tier 3: The Enterprise Information Services Layer

The third tier in our logical architecture is the enterprise information services or data services layer. This layer of the architecture is the most varied and the one about which we can say the least. It is here where portals and other Web-based applications meet the rest of an organization's information infrastructure. Some of the systems found in this tier include the following:

- Relational databases
- ERP systems
- CRM systems
- Sales force automation systems
- Document management systems
- E-mail systems
- Legacy applications

The application server tier is primarily responsible for interfacing with these enterprise components, and together both of these tiers are responsible for transactional integrity and system security. The details of these tasks are discussed in Chapter 3.

## Conclusion

The logical architecture of successful portals consists of three tiers:

1. Presentation layer
2. Application server
3. Enterprise information services

The presentation tier is responsible for rendering content for users and supporting other elements of the user interface. The application server tier is the workhorse of portal applications. It responds to activity in the user interface as well as accesses the data tier to implement the business logic required by portal systems. The enterprise information services tier acts as logical data repositories for portals although these systems themselves can be even more complex than the rest of the portal application.

This division of labor hides the complexity of each tier from the others. This time-tested design principle provides portal designers with the flexibility to combine independent applications without concern for each system's internal implementation details. With the ability to integrate multiple applications in a logical framework and to access those applications from a single interface, we can provide systems modeled after the way we work rather than modeled after implementation details.

## Reference

Britton, Chris. 2001. *Architectures and Middleware: Strategies for Building Large, Integrated Systems.* Boston, MA: Addison-Wesley.

# CHAPTER THREE

# Using a Framework for Application Integration

In this chapter we examine the implementation options for the application server and enterprise information services tiers introduced in Chapter 2. First, we discuss the two application development standards that have emerged as the de facto frameworks for developing Web-based applications: Java 2 Enterprise Edition (J2EE) and Microsoft .NET. These standards provide an overall structure for programmers and designers to build and integrate fine-grained portal components. Next, we examine a coarser-grained level of service, application integration services. These services provide data interchange between systems in the portal. Of course, any time we have movement of data or user access to data, we must provide a security mechanism to control those activities. The section on portal integrity addresses access controls and security standards relevant to enterprise portals. The case study near the end of the chapter describes how one organization used layered architecture and enterprise application integration to meet the diverse needs of its customers.

## The Java 2 Enterprise Edition Framework

The J2EE standard is widely adopted by portal vendors and application providers for its platform independence and its broad range of APIs for distributed computing. The standard is comprised of four basic types of objects:

1. Containers
2. Components
3. Services
4. Connectors

Each of these objects, described briefly in the subsections below, contributes a required piece of the J2EE framework.

## Containers

Containers, as the name implies, house components and services. Transparent to users, containers offer some of the same services provided by operating systems in client/server environments, such as object management and security. Containers also provide housekeeping operations, including transaction support and object-naming services.

In addition, containers manage the start-up and destruction of beans—persistent objects that respond to specific programmatic events according to a set of methods, or procedures, associated with the bean. Beans are one type of component (see below) and are basic building blocks used to create applications or lighter-weight, Web-oriented applets.

## Components

Components are objects that implement application functionality. Components are executed within containers and perform most of the work we associate with an application, like creating the user interface, enforcing business rules, and updating data stores. Four commonly used components in J2EE are listed below:

1. Applications
2. Java Server Pages (JSPs)
3. Servlets
4. Enterprise JavaBeans (EJBs)

These components distribute the workload between server and Web client and provide both single-user and pooled resources.

Application clients are full Java applications analogous to clients in client/server models. Full Java applications provide more functionality than applets, which run within a browser, and servlets, which run on a server. Applications are used for feature-rich, complex applications, such as an OLAP tool.

JSPs are scripting components that allow developers to separate the static and dynamic elements of HTML pages (Figure 3.1). For example, a Web page can contain a basic "Thank you for purchasing . . ." message coded in HTML along with JSP expressions to list the names of the products just ordered by the user. JSPs also allow the HTML coder to reference JavaBeans that encapsulate shared display logic used across a number of pages. JSP is one method for keeping the display and processing logic separated. It also provides the means to shift some of the computing from the server to the client machine. In some cases, though, it is more advantageous to keep the processing on the centralized server; for that purpose, servlets are used.

Servlets are programs that run on the server and generate output based on information passed from a user. Servlets were developed as an improvement over traditional Common Gateway Interface (CGI) programs. CGI provided the first widely used method for getting beyond the static page limits of HTML and

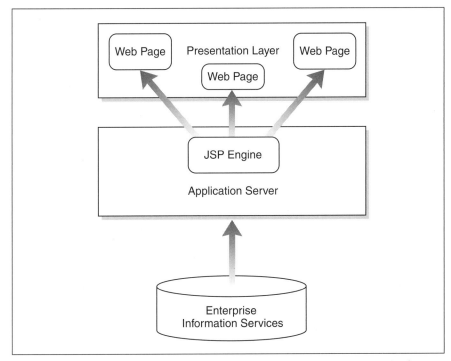

**Figure 3.1    Java Server Pages execute at the application layer and mix HTML and Java code to manage the display of content.**

bridging the Web with back-end processes and databases. However, CGI does have its limits. The biggest problem is that CGI is not very efficient—every time a CGI program is used, a new process is started on the Web server. Servlets avoid the extra overhead of CGI by keeping a single instance of the program in memory and sharing it among multiple users. Like JSPs, servlets generate dynamic HTML code. Servlets are Java programs that can access external processes and databases through standard Java APIs.

With full access to Java, servlets can embody basic business logic for a single application. EJBs were designed for more complex business logic shared across multiple applications.

EJBs are used to implement operations at the business-process level, such as performing credit checks and determining eligibility for insurance coverage. There are two types of EJBs: entity enterprise beans and session beans. Entity enterprise beans maintain persistence and work with a single entity, user, or object on behalf of multiple clients. These are often used to provide access to data from a relational database. Session beans, on the other hand, are used to represent a particular client session on the server. Only stateful session beans maintain state information about the client; stateless beans do not. Information managed by a session bean is lost when the server shuts down so entity beans are used when that data must be available persistently.

## Services

Containers and components are the building blocks of J2EE applications, and services are the glue that keeps them together. Java services target specific processing problems, for example, transporting content and rendering metadata to a display device, updating a database, ensuring that messages sent from one application are actually received by another, and invoking another service required to complete a business process. Some of the most important services used in J2EE applications are listed below.

- *HTTP/HTTPS*: These transport protocols are used for displaying Web content. HTTPS is the secure counterpart of HTTP.
- *Java Naming and Directory Interface (JNDI)*: This service provides the means to locate other components in a distributed system.
- *Java Database Connectivity (JDBC)*: The JDBC API is a database interface, similar in some ways to the ODBC interface used in some client/server applications.

- *Java Message Service (JMS)*: Distributed processes require the ability to send point-to-point and publish/subscribe messages. JMS provides enterprise-scale messaging, similar to the type found in mainframe operations using IBM's MQ Series messaging services.
- *JavaMail*: This service supports programmatic access to e-mail services.
- *Java Transaction API (JTA and JTS)*: Transaction support is essential in many distributed applications. For example, to maintain accurate inventory levels, the inventory management system must be updated each time an order is placed or shipped. Making sure the order processing and inventory management systems stay in synch is the responsibility of the transaction management service.
- *Remote Method Invocation/Internet Inter-ORB Protocol (RMI/IIOP)*: The RMI/IIOP service is a protocol for invoking services and programs on separate servers.

The extensible J2EE framework already supports a number of services, and if needs should arise for others, the standard can easily accommodate them.

## Connectors

The J2EE standard also specifies the J2EE Connector Architecture, a framework for linking the application server layer with the enterprise information services layer. The purpose of this component is to provide a standard mechanism for accessing databases, ERP systems, CRM systems, and legacy applications, among others. To do this the J2EE Connector Architecture defines an object called a resource adapter.

Resource adapters must work with J2EE application servers on the one hand and with external applications on the other. Interactions between application server components and an EIS occur through the adapter interface. The Common Client Interface (CCI) is a generic interface to different types of EIS applications. The CCI includes objects and methods for connecting and interacting with the EIS, retrieving and updating data, and querying metadata about the EIS. In addition to the interface elements, the adapter must provide services transparent to the developer, such as connection pooling, transaction support, and security controls. Figure 3.2 shows the logical structure of the Connector Architecture.

The combination of containers, components, services, and connectors is a powerful and flexible architecture for building portal applications. However, it is

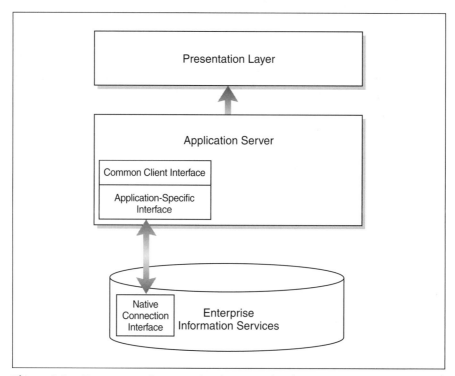

**Figure 3.2    Resource adapters plug into application servers following J2EE standard requirements and into enterprise information systems using native protocols and programming interfaces.**

not the only game in town. The other major architectural standard, Microsoft .NET, builds on the strengths of the Windows family of operating systems and related applications.

## The Microsoft .NET Architecture

The .NET architecture from Microsoft is centered on Web services. Like J2EE, .NET has clients, servers, and access to EISs. Unlike J2EE, there is not a single application server framework around which business applications are deployed. Instead, Microsoft offers a set of .NET Servers that meet particular needs. Microsoft's architecture is not tied to a single language like J2EE; developers are free to choose from many different programming languages when building .NET applications.

## Web Services

Web services, the heart of Microsoft's architectural approach, are applications that expose their functionality to other applications through an XML interface. Unlike other distributed processing methods, Web services neither require binary-level compatibility nor make assumptions about the implementation language. SOAP is the XML protocol for invoking Web services and exchanging information between them. The Web Services Description Language (WSDL) and Universal Discovery Description and Integration (UDDI) provide additional details and locating information for using Web services. With a simple but expressive XML protocol like SOAP, the barriers to integration are significantly reduced when compared to earlier distributed procedure calling methods. This in turn provides the foundation for integrating different types of servers.

## .NET Servers

The .NET Enterprise Servers include the following:

- Windows 2000 and Windows .NET, the underlying operating system
- Application Center 2000, a basis for building scalable Web applications
- BizTalk Server 2000, an enterprise application integration platform
- Commerce Server, an e-commerce applications server
- Content Management Server, a content system for dynamic e-business
- Exchange Servers, a messaging and collaboration server
- Host Integration, a gateway for mainframe integration
- Internet Security and Acceleration Server, a system for additional Internet security
- Mobile Information Sever, a server for delivering content to mobile devices
- SharePoint Portal Server, a server for finding and publishing unstructured content
- SQL Server, a relational database

The functionality of these servers is accessed through custom applications developed with Active Server Pages (ASPs) and programming languages built on Microsoft's Common Language Runtime (CLR).

Moving to a higher level of application integration, we will now examine enterprise application integration methods.

## Application Integration Services

The hallmark of a portal is integration. Portals provide single points of access to applications across the enterprise. These applications all function within the integrated framework of the portal but to varying degrees. At one end of the spectrum we have shallow integration, which brings applications together at the interface level. For example, utility applications (such as those that provide stock quotes, airline schedules, and currency converters) are all accessible from a single location in the portal and so, in a limited sense, are integrated within the portal framework. The applications themselves do not exchange data or in any way depend on each other—they simply coexist in close proximity within the user interface. The more interesting examples of EAI use a deeper level of interoperation and are the focus of this section. The challenges and benefits of application integration occur behind the scenes of the portal interface, where we find architecture and process issues that are as old as information technology (IT) itself.

The business driver behind integration is the fact that multiple IT systems are often required to complete a single business operation. For example, accepting an order online from a customer could require a series of steps that use or update information in inventory, customer billing, and fulfillment databases. The ease with which the online order is filled depends on how these systems were designed, how the enterprise has grown, and how business processes have changed. In the ideal world, these distinct systems would be designed with the current business processes in mind and with an eye to integration with other applications. This is rarely the case. Changing business models, mergers, and other competitive pressures constantly force organizations to rethink their operations. Portals are one of the arrows in the IT quiver to help implement business strategies, and EAI is an essential element of those portals.

Application integration is not a new IT process, but the methods for conducting EAI are becoming better understood. In the past, point-to-point integration was often used to exchange data between applications. For example, if an underwriting system needed data from a claims processing system, a custom data exchange would be built. If a billing system needed information from the same claims processing system, another exchange would be built, and so on for any other application that needed data from the source system. The limitations of this architecture are obvious. The number of exchanges grows with each new point of integration, and each of these needs to be maintained. A single change in a source system can cause ripple-effect changes to any or all of the exchanges. A better approach is to standardize on a middleware model in which applications serve data to a middleware broker or mechanism that is responsible for getting the data to its ultimate destination in the appropriate format. (See the sidebar Multichannel Integration at the Institute for Healthcare Improvement in Chapter 6.)

Middleware for enterprise information exchange is essential for many portal applications. The promise of portals, that is, the efficiency gained by using a single point of access to multiple business processes and applications, depends on the systems' ability to complete logical business processes regardless of the underlying application architecture. For example, a customer making an order online does not need to be aware of inventory, fulfillment, and billing systems. To isolate the users from implementation details that are irrelevant from their perspective and to ensure that the integrity of business processes is respected, portal applications depend on EAI techniques. EAI systems provide two core functions: the ability to create messages that are meaningful to both source and target systems and the ability to guarantee the delivery of messages between systems.

## EAI Architectures

You can design the middleware for application integration using two different models: the hub-and-spoke model and the messaging model.

### The Hub-and-Spoke Model

The hub-and-spoke model, as shown in Figure 3.3, provides a central routing server (the hub) that accepts messages from clients (the spokes) and routes them to the destination (another spoke). The advantage of this model is that senders and receivers do not need to know details of the other implementation. If one client changes, only the hub needs to accommodate the change, not the other client applications.

The main drawback of this model is that the hub can quickly become a bottleneck and a single point of failure. Several alternative models have been proposed [Linthicum 2001]:

- Federated static
- Federated dynamic
- Transactional
- Peer-to-peer
- Hybrid

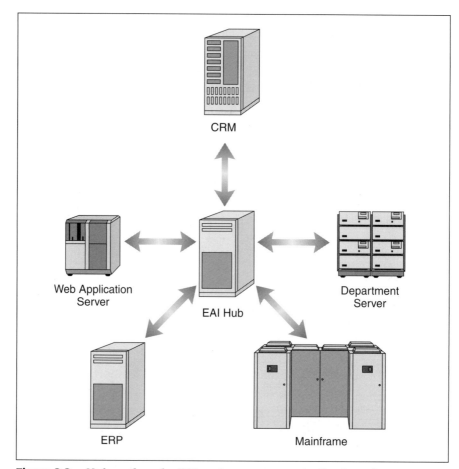

CRM

Web Application
Server

EAI Hub

Department
Server

ERP

Mainframe

**Figure 3.3    Hub-and-spoke EAI systems use a centralized routing server.**

Federated static architectures use multiple hubs each processing the message load for a set of applications and communicating with the other hubs. Since applications bind to a single hub, this approach does not provide load balancing. The federated dynamic model uses multiple hubs but also provides for sharing the processing load between servers. Transactional architectures perform data exchange operations within the context of atomic transactions and use server resources more efficiently than other EAI models. They do not work well in asynchronous environments where message brokers are more appropriate. Peer-to-peer models use server-based agents, instead of central servers, to process and route messages. This is the newest of the models and while promising, it does not have the track record of some of the older, more established models. Hybrid models combine features from two or more of the first four models. As Linthicum [2001] points out, the combination of transactional and hub-and-spoke models provides resource sharing with asynchronous, event-driven message processing.

*The Messaging Model*

Messaging systems, as demonstrated in Figure 3.4, use a bus model rather than the centralized server of the hub-and-spoke model. When applications exchange data, the source system creates a message with the relevant data and submits it to a queue, which guarantees its delivery. The main elements of a messaging system are listed below.

• Adapters or gateways
• Metadata directory
• Message queue
• Audit trail database
• Routing service
• Transformation and mapping services

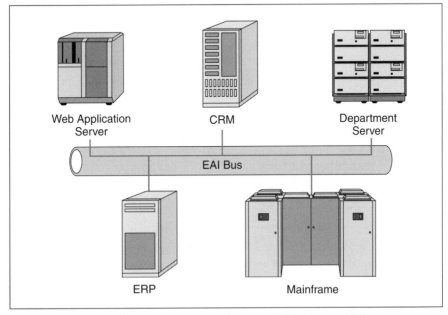

**Figure 3.4    Messaging systems use a bus model for transmitting messages.**

Adapters are application-specific connectors that link applications to the message broker. The metadata directory maintains information about systems by using messaging services and supports message reformatting and delivery. The message queue is the heart of the messaging system and is responsible for accepting messages and ensuring they are delivered. The audit trail database records messages sent through the system for later reporting and analysis. The routing service supports additional functionality beyond basic queuing, such as publish and subscribe services. Transformation and mapping services reformat messages to ensure they are syntactically acceptable to the target system.

Some messaging systems, such as IBM's MQ Series, are applications themselves while others, such as the Java Message Service API, are service components on which other applications are built.

### Characteristics of EAI Systems

In addition to variations in architecture, EAI systems are distinguished by a number of other characteristics. Some EAI applications are loosely coupled while others are tightly coupled. Loosely coupled systems tend to operate fairly independently and exchange relatively small amounts of information. Tightly coupled systems depend more heavily on each other and share more data than loosely coupled systems do. The more tightly coupled the systems, the more constrained the business process that dictates the exchange. Loosely coupled systems are more easily integrated. From the perspective of a portal user, the loosely versus tightly coupled exchange is transparent; it is the portal application designer who must understand and address the implications.

Another distinguishing characteristic of these applications is whether they are synchronous or asynchronous. In the former case, the source system must wait for a transaction to complete on the target system before proceeding. This is a potential bottleneck and can constrain the source system unnecessarily. Asynchronous messaging, on the other hand, does not require the source system to wait for the target system to complete an operation. This allows for greater flexibility in design and eliminates a potential slowdown in source system processing. For example, a customer placing an order online will need to wait while credit is verified, so the synchronous model is appropriate. Sending order information to a billing system can be done asynchronously because a response from the billing system is not needed immediately.

EAI is an underlying technology that allows us to implement entire business processes within a portal. As we shall see later in the chapter in the Empire Blue

Cross Blue Shield case study, EAI is the glue that holds complex business processes together. Building portal applications within an EAI framework allows for greater flexibility in business processes and minimizes the impact of changes in one area of business (e.g., billing systems) on other dependent areas.

## Protecting the Integrity of the Portal

### Single Sign-On, Identity Management, and Provisioning

Portal users have the benefit of single-point access to multiple applications. In some cases, application integration can mitigate the need to use multiple systems by combining multiple business operations into a single operation. In most cases, however, users still need to access multiple applications from across the enterprise; traditionally this has meant managing multiple passwords. Help desk agents experience increases in call volume as demands for password resets inevitably increase. But the need for access controls should not be underestimated. According to Datamonitor [2002], 42% of security breaches in 2000 were unauthorized internal and external accesses to enterprise systems. To balance the ease of user access with the security demands of organizations, many enterprises are turning to single sign-on systems.

A single sign-on system allows a user to authenticate once to a centralized security system that manages the user's passwords for other applications. For example, a user may log into a single sign-on server through the portal and navigate to a CRM system. The CRM system has its own access control mechanism and requires the user to log in. When the CRM system challenges the user for credentials, the single sign-on server intercepts the challenge and provides the user's credentials to the application. The user is granted his or her appropriate access to the CRM system without having to remember or provide another username and password.

The advantages of single sign-on affect several parts of the organization. Portal users have easier access to the tools they need. System administrators improve security by reducing the likelihood of passwords scribbled on notes taped to monitors. Single sign-on servers can also enforce a password policy to prevent users from choosing easily guessed passwords, keeping the same password for too long a time, or repeatedly using the same password. Help desk support calls, which cost an average of $32 per call [Taylor 2002], are reduced.

To fully solve the access control problem in enterprise-scale applications, single sign-on needs to incorporate additional authorization and provisioning services. These systems are typically referred to as identity management systems. Identity management and provisioning applications offer several features.

- Single sign-on for Web applications is the most important reason to use these systems.
- Centralized access control policies dictate which users can access content and applications and when that access can occur. Policies are built on rules and roles. Rules describe restrictions on the use of resources, such as servers and printers, and on the operations users can perform. Roles are groups of users who share a particular set of rights. Rules provide fine-grained control over resources, and roles ease administration of enterprise security. The best single sign-on products support both.
- Self-service allows users to create and manage their own credentials without the need for administrators or help desk agents. Initially, users have to disclose some information known only to the user and the organization to create an account. From that point, users can manage their own identities and profiles.
- A secure database stores passwords for multiple applications and provides them to applications when users are challenged for authentication. This process is handled transparently to users.
- In addition to authentication, identity management systems should provide auditing and reporting functions for administrators.

Single sign-on and identity management systems face a number of implementation challenges. The provisioning system that manages accounts must be secured. As gatekeeper to multiple systems, these systems are obvious targets for hackers. A second challenge is integration with legacy systems. Some single sign-on systems work only with Web-enabled applications, and custom integration may be required. A workflow element is needed to manage the approval process as users request new or modified permissions. Also, these systems typically have to deal with communicating across heterogeneous platforms. This may become easier as standards are adopted.

### Standards for Sharing Security Requirements

A number of standards, briefly listed below, are in place and evolving to meet access control requirements in distributed environments.

- *Secure Socket Layer (SSL) and Transport Layer Security (TLS)*: These are probably the most widely adopted security standards used on the Web. SSL and its successor, TLS, provide a secure channel of communication between two processes, such as a client browser making a purchase and a Web server executing the transaction at a vendor site. SSL and TLS use certificates provided by trusted third parties to ensure that client processes are actually communicating with authentic sites and not rogue servers set up to look like legitimate sites.

- *XML Encryption:* This standard provides a mechanism to encrypt some information in a document while leaving other parts unencrypted. It also supports secure communication between multiple parties.
- *XML Digital Signatures (XML-DSIG):* This standard allows authors to digitally sign XML documents by using public key infrastructure (PKI) technology.
- *Web Services Security (WS-Security):* This protocol uses SOAP messages to transmit security information, such as identity and authorization data. It builds on the XML Encryption and XML-DSIG standards.
- *Service Provisioning Markup Language (SPML):* This markup language supports the exchange of resource and provisioning information in Web services environments.
- *Security Assertion Markup Language (SAML):* This XML standard supports the exchange of security information about entities (that is, people and computers) in an application context. The information is in the form of assertions about what access rights an entity has in a particular context.
- *XML Key Management Specification (XKMS):* This standard addresses the exchange of public keys used with XML signatures.

You can find more information on these and other emerging e-business standards at the OASIS site at http://www.oasis-open.org/.

---

**CASE STUDY:  Empire Blue Cross Blue Shield Brings It All Together**

Founded in 1934, Empire Blue Cross Blue Shield is the largest health insurance company in the state of New York based on PPO and HMO membership. The company maintained six independent membership, claims processing, and billing systems by the mid-1990s due to acquiring different lines of business. In 1995, Empire began consolidating its claims systems into two enterprise systems. Leveraging these enterprise systems enabled deployment of the company's customer-centric portals beginning in 1999.

With these portals, Empire has reduced the time required to develop new proposals from 25–30 days to 2–3 days for brokers. Physicians can now accurately process member claims in real time, with over 90% of these transactions correctly handled in the first pass. The goal of the portals targeted for customers is to make the most frequently requested transactions available by phone, fax, mail, or Web and thus substitute a completely automated process for one requiring human intervention.

### The Problem: Multiple Customers, Multiple Systems

To understand customer portals in the health care industry, we first have to understand that there is no single type of customer; there are *four*.

1. Members and their families insured individually or through their employers
2. Physicians (the providers) who are concerned about members' eligibility, benefits, and reimbursement for their services
3. Brokers who sell insurance to employers on behalf of insurers and work closely with insurance companies to enroll members
4. Employers who provide health insurance coverage to their employees

Each of these customers has distinct needs and expectations so Empire has developed separate portals for each. Each portal, however, is developed on the same architectural framework, which is centered on a richly integrated information infrastructure. The integrated infrastructure provides the foundation for meeting the single most important aspect of a customer portal:

> *The user experience must be designed from the user's perspective and not driven by the implementation of underlying systems.*

For example, eligibility criteria may be managed by one system and claims processing by another, but members will need information from both when they inquire about rejected claims. For members, the issue is about coverage and eligibility for medical treatment; it is not about business processes such as claims processing. Those are internal issues, and the surrounding details, while ultimately important to the user, are irrelevant to the user experience. The Empire portals accommodate the user experience by treating the user, not the applications, as the center of interaction.

**The Solution: Layered Architecture and Enterprise Application Integration**

Ultimately, user interactions translate into transactions—claims are processed and payments are made. To map from a logically customer-centric interface to an application-centric transaction processing model, Empire used a layered design consisting of four layers:

1. Systems layer
2. Framework layer
3. Business component layer
4. Application layer

The foundation, the systems layer, includes reusable objects that encapsulate basic operations, such as message delivery. The insurer depends on a number of standards for systems-layer objects, including HTTP/XML, JMS, JDBC, and EJBs. The systems layer is responsible for back-end processing such as submitting IMS transactions and relaying the response back to the initiating operation. Application-specific code is effectively encapsulated within the systems layer, which uses XML documents to receive and send information from the framework layer.

The framework layer builds on the systems-level components to deliver basic business process services such as Web personalization and transaction workflow. These services in turn are used by the business component level to implement higher-level business processes such as determining eligibility, processing claims, and managing correspondence. Interactions between the layers are optimized based on user behavior. For example, separate queries to the enterprise system collect member-related data and summarize claim data and detailed data about a specific claim. The business component layer then selects and reorganizes the data to meet multiple requirements in the application layer. The application layer includes interfaces designed for each of the four customer types described earlier.

Integrating and managing these layers required some additions to the existing infrastructure. Early in the design phases, the development team decided to build to the J2EE standard, using Web application servers and messaging middleware into the enterprise architecture. IBM's WebSphere server manages the business layer, IBM's HTTP server manages the presentation layer, and IBM MQ Series provides messaging services between constituent applications. A separate Lightweight Directory Access Protocol LDAP server manages user authentication while an Oracle database manages transient session-oriented data.

The multilayered architecture allows Empire to deliver real-time access to transaction processing systems over the Web and is clearly a technological success—but at first it still did not meet all of the customers' needs. Many aspects of the enterprise application were originally designed for customer service representatives (CSRs) and other internal users. These CSRs receive extensive training and have access to other resources within the company for performing core tasks, for example, processing claims and determining eligibility. Members and physicians do not. The insurer could not simply expose the enterprise system, as is, over the Web. Instead, Empire leveraged the intellectual capital from CSR training material about interpreting codes and mapped it to an XML representation. This interpretive information was made explicitly available to portal users to allow them to better understand the context of their transaction. Empire focused on the customer experience and adapted the portal application to meet the users' needs rather than designing the portal around the structure of the underlying application.

## Best Practices

The Empire Blue Cross Blue Shield team members used several best practices in the development of the portal.

- **First and foremost, keep a customer-centric focus.** The portals were designed around the customer experience as opposed to simply reflecting the underlying implementation of an existing system. The insurer also made a concerted effort to publicize the portals. The marketing plan included messages on interactive voice response systems directing callers to the Web, in renewal mailings, and in Explanation of Benefits documents. The team never assumed a "build it and they will come" position.
- **Decouple applications through the use of messaging middleware and standardize on an XML document type for transactions.** This mechanism isolates changes in underlying systems from affecting other constituent applications in the portal. A change in the claims processing system will not ripple through the architecture requiring changes, for example, to the presentation layer.

- **Use a layered approach to provide for component reuse across applications.** The systems, framework, and business component layers all serve the requirements of four distinct portals. A clean separation of low-level tasks (e.g., data access and workflow control) from business-level operations (e.g., claims processing) ensures that new business processes can be easily accommodated within the framework by using existing low-level services.
- **Use standards-based solutions.** Although their back-end systems are built on proprietary IBM platforms such as IMS, functions outside the systems layer are based on standard solutions such as XML and JDBC.
- **Roll out incrementally.** The team rolled out the portals in a phased implementation, starting with the broker portal in October 2000 and then moving to the member portal in December 2000, followed in 2001 by the physician and employer portals in August and December, respectively. The team did not try to deliver the entire suite of portals at once, but the speed at which the second, third, and fourth portals were delivered speaks to the efficacy of layered architectures and component reuse.

By designing well-integrated reusable components, Empire Blue Cross Blue Shield has met diverse customer requirements today and created a framework for future expansion.

Content used with permission of Empire Blue Cross.

## Conclusion

One of the defining characteristics of portals is application integration. To effectively integrate existing applications and accommodate future changes and additions, it is imperative that we design with logical frameworks in mind. Many in the IT industry are currently designing distributed applications using the J2EE and .NET platforms. These standards provide a wide range of services, from messaging to security. The J2EE standard is application dependent while the .NET model is based on specific Microsoft applications. Both are designed to provide scalable, reliable services in a distributed environment—ideal for the enterprise portal.

As portal applications become more complex and address wide-ranging business processes, we need to integrate multiple systems. We could design custom integration systems each time we need to move data from one system to another. However, this quickly would become a design and maintenance headache, to say the least. EAI frameworks, like the hub-and-spoke model and the messaging model, offer a superior alternative. Data moves between applications in controlled manners, transactions are managed across applications, and the framework adopts more easily to change than with ad hoc point-to-point solutions.

## References

Datamonitor. 2002. *Single Sign-On: Enterprise Access Made Secure and Easy*. Accessed in June 2003 at *http://www3.ca.com/Files/IndustryAnalystReports/SSO.pdf*.

Linthicum, David S. 2001. "Making EAI Scale." *Intelligent Enterprise*, April 16. Accessed in June 2003 at *http://www.intelligenteai.com/feature/010416/linthicum.shtml*.

Taylor, Laura. 2002. "Understanding Single Sign-On." *Intranet.com*, May 28. Accessed in June 2003 at *http://www.intranetjournal.com/articles/200205/se_05_28_02a.html*.

# CHAPTER FOUR

# Ensuring
# Portal Adoption

Enterprise information portals (EIPs) have the potential to change the way we work but only if they are adopted by end users. Throughout this book we will see examples of flexible, integrated portal applications. Portal vendors and software developers provide us with the tools to deliver compelling applications based on the sound design principles discussed in earlier chapters. The success or failure of portal deployments also hinges on nontechnical issues. How well portal components are deployed to meet business objectives and how well they fit into users' ways of working are key factors in the ultimate success of a portal.

In this chapter we examine several best practices that promote adoption by end users. We also examine a few common reasons for poor acceptance of these systems. The chapter concludes with a case study on CARE Canada's highly successful knowledge management portal, which realized high adoption.[1]

## Best Practices for Ensuring Portal Adoption

Portals vary widely in their design, application, and use, but successful portal projects seem to share a number of

[1] This chapter is based largely on a series of articles written for *DM Review* [Aiken and Sullivan 2002, Sullivan 2002a, and Sullivan 2002b]. Used here with permission of *DM Review*.

common characteristics, especially with regard to adoption. Well-used portals often result from teams that:

- Address business processes as well as content management and access to applications
- Share decision making about management of the portal
- Support both formal and informal modes of collaboration
- Adapt to changing needs
- Deploy with clear communications about the purpose of the portal
- Provide compelling reasons for users to use the portal
- Tackle comparatively easy problems before undertaking more difficult objectives

Each of these best practices contributes to the adoption puzzle that must be addressed in every portal project if it is to succeed. The following subsections examine each of these practices in more depth.

**Support Business Processes**

Portal deployments should account for how information is used, how it changes over time, and how it can be accessed and manipulated.

For example, product managers regularly have to report on production performance, resource utilization, costs, and other tactical issues. Each of these areas can require several different reports from the data warehouse along with background material kept in document management systems. Ideally, the portal manages not only access to the information in these performance reports but also the process of gathering and sharing it with the end consumers of the information. Workflow or collaboration systems can eliminate ad hoc substitutes for structured information sharing. For example, without a workflow system, many users find themselves downloading reports and documents from a portal, compressing them, and e-mailing the package to the next person in the organizational chain. A simpler method would be to have users review content within the portal, approve it for further review, and have a workflow system manage the operation of sending that information to the next person in the process.

Many portal systems provide workflow management services that can support business processes. Workflows are frequently used to manage the publishing of content to a portal. Authors submit their content to a specific portal area, and it is automatically sent to the editor responsible for that section of the portal. When approved by the editor, the workflow system automatically publishes the content to the site. More complex routing schemes and business rules may be required for many processes, but these applications are still well suited for portal implementations. Insurance claims processing, press release reviews, contract approvals, and project reporting processes can all use controlled management through a variety of states from the start of the process to completion.

This best practice is rooted in the understanding that information available in a portal must often be acted upon by different users, at different times, and under different conditions. Embedding the business rules that govern these types of processes in a workflow management system will relieve users of these repetitive, error-prone operations.

## Share Decision Making

Enterprise information portals touch too many organizational and technical points of an enterprise to depend on centralized decision making. At the same time, organizations need to maintain some level of control over infrastructure and design issues. The choices of portal software, business intelligence tools, and single sign-on services, for example, are best centralized into one decision-making body. Basic navigation and labeling frameworks are best standardized across the organization, although department- or team-based adaptations should be accommodated. The design of navigation taxonomies should be shared between enterprise, business unit, and department levels with each defining categories for its own domain but leaving detailed classification choices (e.g., directory and taxonomy layers lower than three levels deep) to lower-level units. This type of federated model balances the need for governing frameworks while allowing business units and departments to make choices appropriate for their areas.

There is no single federated model that we can point to as the ideal example. Every organization is different and will need to find a balanced model of decision making that reflects its organizational nature. We can, however, consider some of the most salient characteristics of well-designed governance models.

First, governance models address a minimal set of requirements including the following:

- Security provisions
- Metadata standards
- Search capabilities
- Directory and taxonomy development
- Navigation patterns
- Usability issues

These services and standards are all shared throughout the portal and, for ease of use, should be consistent throughout the portal.

Second, governance models should not delve into what is published (that is the province of content authors and application administrators); nor should models address how services are provided (that should be left to system administrators and architects). For example, governing bodies should define the features required of a search engine but leave it to technical evaluation teams to choose the tool that best meets those needs.

Third, governance models should be multitiered, and the scope of each tier should be limited both in the breadth and depth of its decision making. The goal of the federated model is to create a minimal framework that ensures interoperability, security, a consistent user experience, and high-quality search and navigation services.

### Provide for Formal and Informal Collaboration

With knowledge sharing as a key driver for many portals, support for collaboration among users is essential. Two modes of collaboration are emerging as common models in portal implementations. The first is the document-centric approach in which information and knowledge are captured, formally recorded, and added to content repositories. The second approach focuses on informal communications between individuals, as typified by the proverbial conversation at the water cooler. Both approaches have their benefits and neither meets, by itself, the full range of knowledge management needs in most organizations.

Document-centric approaches leverage the benefits of written language: Information is preserved over time, it is easily transmitted and shared with many people, and it is readily revised and corrected. These are exactly the characteristics we need for successful management and development of complex processes like creating new product lines, overseeing large projects, and standardizing quality control measures over multiple facilities. A well-developed document-centric model also includes informal documents, such as e-mail messages and threaded discussions. The benefits of document-centric collaboration are that core information and knowledge are readily disseminated throughout the organization. The downside is that no matter how extensive the documentation, it can never give a complete picture of decision-making processes, capture the mistakes and missed opportunities, or convey the hard truths that some would rather not have in writing. Of course, sometimes we just need a short, fast answer, not a dissertation. This is where informal communications come in.

Informal collaboration tools have few rules that govern their use. Discussion groups, for example, are organized by topic and often open to a relatively broad audience, such as everyone in a company or all the members of a project team. Informal communications between discussion group members range from questions about technical issues (e.g., "What does Oracle error TNS-12531 mean?") to brief postings about a decision made by someone on a team (e.g., "I'm changing several assumptions in the new sales projection model."). Even without detailed rules for use, discussion groups often evolve into particular functions, such as a log of problem-solving activities or histories of project activities. Without formal direction, portal users create informal knowledge-sharing repositories. Complementing these grassroots-driven collaboration tools are centralized expertise directories.

Users can find better answers and get them faster by talking with an expert directly (if they know whom they can turn to) rather than searching and browsing portal content. This is particularly true when the question posed is well defined (e.g., "What is the best way to restart the extrusion process after one of the feed lines has been contaminated?" or "We're planning to use component A in the new product, but you used component B in the earlier version. Why?"). In situations like these, the portal's role is to provide a directory of expertise.

Compiling such a directory is a time-intensive task, primarily due to personnel and organizational issues. To get a rapid return on investment (ROI), start with people who understand high-valued operations, for example, engineers who understand production operations and can help front-line operators diagnose disruptive problems, or market analysts who have in-depth knowledge about target markets. Being an expert does not require a Ph.D. and several patents. More important is firsthand or in-depth knowledge of a subject important to the organization and a willingness to field inquiries from others. Document the experts' areas of expertise and make the directory easy to search. Include detailed references to specific projects they worked on and, of course, keep the directory up-to-date.

When creating expertise directories, be prepared for unanticipated organizational issues. For example, will including someone in the directory change his or her position or status, especially relative to collective bargaining? Will organizational walls hinder frank discussions between employees in different parts of the company? What responsibility do experts bear for how their advice is used? Some characteristics of organizational culture can have a chilling effect on the use of internal expertise, but other facets of that culture may promote it, sometimes in unexpected ways. For example, if the content in portal repositories about projects lacks frank discussions about mistakes and failures, users will justifiably question the integrity of the content and turn to other sources of information, such as the experts actually involved in those projects. Also watch out for expert directories that simply reflect formal and informal organizational hierarchies. Does the CIO really need to be included in the list of portal experts simply because the project is in that person's department? The integrity of the expert directory will be diluted if individuals are added for their own benefits and not those of other users.

Portal users need access to a range of information. Sometimes this information is structured in formal documents, sometimes it is several levels down in a discussion thread, and often it isn't written down at all. If a portal offers an avenue to reach each of those information sources, it will be well used.

## Adapt to Changing Needs

Portal users also need to meet changing business needs, which in turn requires the portal to change to meet those needs. To understand whether you are meeting the diverse and changing needs of users you should develop metrics to gauge the portal's effectiveness.

To begin, measure which applications are used and who is using them. For example, human resource applications frequently draw a broad audience because of their access to employee information, but those same applications do not necessarily drive the use of other portal services. Likewise, it is impossible to know without testing whether users come from a cross-section of the organization or from a limited number of departments. Analyzing portal and Web server logs, combined with information about users and organizational units frequently found in enterprise directories, can shed light on who is using which elements of the portal.

If statistics show that an application is underutilized, conduct interviews to learn why. Some common reasons are a lack of integration with other applications (especially desktop tools), difficulties accessing the application because of multiple logins and poor navigation, and lack of relevant content. Users speak frankly in one-on-one interviews. Try to avoid focus group interviews, which can skew the results toward the opinions of just a few members of the group. With a more complete understanding of users' needs, you can adapt portals to changing requirements.

## Market the Portal

Launching a portal is like launching a product. You need to let your target market, the user community, know what you have to offer and why they should consider it. Companies wouldn't think of launching a new product without a marketing campaign. The same should go for enterprise information portals. It is probably safe to assume the ultimate users of the portal are too busy to browse and explore the new system looking for a useful tool or interesting content. As portal developers we need to provide that information directly and succinctly to users. (After all, those most pressed for time are the ones who should benefit the most from the EIP, yet they have the least time to learn about it.)

Successful portals offer concrete benefits. Tedious jobs, like filing timecards and expense reports, are made less time consuming; information is available on demand with minimal delay; the portal provides access to a broad range of information organized according to each user's work context; and most importantly, the information is reliable. Getting the word out about these benefits will help drive adoption, which is the ultimate measure of success. Of course, this type of marketing campaign assumes the portal has something significant to offer.

## Provide Compelling Reasons to Use the Portal

To succeed, enterprise information portals must be crafted to the particular processes of an organization. This means focusing on the issues that demand the time and attention of the end user. The first step in shifting the focus to a grassroots-oriented development model is to recognize that one of the chief reasons EIPs fail to deliver is the lack of a compelling reason to use the portal.

One reason users adopt a portal is to use anchor applications, such as business intelligence report programs, enterprise search engines, collaboration tools, and document repositories. These tools meet multiple needs, cross project and department boundaries, and are tied to core business operations. Siemens' widely publicized ShareNet portal [Red Hat 2002] provides professionals around the world with access to sales proposals and has been responsible for incremental sales in the hundreds of millions of dollars. That is compelling. What's not compelling? The news feeds, corporate messages, and utilities for tracking flight information and converting currencies. While these components are helpful, they do not drive users to the portal.

So what constitutes an anchor application? First, anchor applications support core business processes: selling telecommunications equipment, researching market information, designing new products, and so on. Second, they provide a service not easily available elsewhere. For example, collaborating through a threaded discussion can be done asynchronously and without regard to geography, plus it has the added benefit of creating a record of the dialog that can be referenced at a later time. Project teams can share files through file systems, but Web access and better metadata support are key advantages to using a portal framework. Third, and perhaps most importantly, these applications aid users in their recurring tasks, whether processing insurance claims, developing sales proposals, or tracking production metrics.

To create an anchor application, designers need to observe and understand not only what users do but also how they do it. When Etienne Wenger [1999] observed insurance claims processors in his research on communities of practice, he discovered an elaborate system of processes and artifacts that enabled staff members to get their jobs done. We do not need to become anthropologists to design decent applications, but we do need to understand what information people use in their work and how they interact with others. This can come from detailed observations over an extended period of time, which is impractical in most cases, or by following a grassroots, bottom-up design methodology.

### Tackle Easy Problems First

We can learn a couple of important lessons from well-adopted EIPs. Deploy to the true believers first. Keep the early phases of deployment focused on staff members who understand the potential for the portal and have pressing business needs. For example, find a business situation that is untenable, for example, employees need to follow procedures for a particular process but can't find documentation. In another case, a department might have accumulated too many custom reports over the years; now some are unused, some are forgotten, and many people don't know the reports exist. Replace these with an ad hoc query tool.

Weave the tool into everyday work. A process that requires creating a document in Microsoft Word, logging into a portal, and then proceeding through a three-step wizard to add the document is too tedious a process to be widely adopted. In this case, a WebDAV interface would support a more seamless integration of the desktop and the portal. In general, consider the mechanical process of using the portal and watch for users saying, "There has to be a better way." There usually *is* a better way, and it's often not too difficult to implement.

These best practices are found in many successful portals, and when implemented properly they drive adoption. Just as important, though, is knowing which pitfalls could arise.

## Root Causes of Poor Adoption

Organizations are pouring valuable IT resources into developing and deploying enterprise information portals with clear expectations about ROI. But what if knowledge workers don't use the portal? What if the little-spoken truth behind EIPs is that too often, users don't care? If users do not adopt the portal, much of the ROI is not realized; users continue to rely on alternative, less efficient methods to get their jobs done; and IT ends up maintaining the portal as well as the ad hoc substitutes for a centralized data and content management system. To avoid this problem, we need to understand it.

Poor adoption can strike any portal project. The list below outlines the most common causes.

- The portal is difficult to use.
- Users question the integrity of portal content.
- The project lacks executive or user sponsorship (or both).
- The user community suffers from organizational inertia and aversion to change.

The subsections below discuss each of these in turn.

### Poor Usability

Ease of use and usability have been the focus of much debate. We've all seen lists of the best and worst Web sites and have been admonished at conferences, seminars, and training classes to pay attention to how customers actually use a site. The customers for EIPs are primarily knowledge workers who use such portals to locate information, find people, and share information. We shouldn't forget that users have alternative methods for performing these tasks; if another option is faster or more trustworthy than the portal, our customers have no reason to use the portal.

Take a simple example. Suppose you're an engineer designing a component and you have a problem with heat dissipation. You think some engineers on another team had a similar problem with a different type of component, and you want to find out who solved the problem and how they did it. You could (a) search the portal for "heat dissipation problem," (b) scan old public e-mail folders looking for similar problems, or (c) get on the phone and start dialing for answers. In too many cases the most likely route to success is (c), followed by (b), with (a) a distant third. What are we doing wrong here?

First, most portal search tools are effectively useless because we don't invest the time required to configure them properly. This is the product of an "it works out of the box" mentality. The truth is that searching is complicated. If we download a search tool from the Web, run the crawlers, and start firing off queries like "heat dissipation problem," we'll get hits—all four thousand of them. The first step toward successful searches is finding content that meets the search criteria. The second and often forgotten step is organizing the content in such a way that users can find what they really need. This requires categorization and taxonomies, which take time to develop. It also requires careful attention to metadata, the foundation of parametric searching (e.g., "restrict searching to documents written by a particular author, between these dates, and with a document type 'engineering analysis'"). The problem lies not with the search tools (well, sometimes it does) but with how we use them.

A related problem is making sure we provide access to information wherever it may be. Enterprise searches cannot be restricted to portal content—they must include shared network drives, public e-mail folders, document management systems, industry-related sites, and partners' Web sites. Searching is now a whole lot harder, but the point is to give our customers, the knowledge workers, what they need, not just what is easy to deploy. We must be careful not to fall into the trap of checking off search functions from a list of portal requirements and assuming we are done because the work has just begun to create a usable system.

## Concerns about Content Integrity

A second cause of poor adoption is a perceived lack of content integrity. In some cases, users do not believe they can actually access what they need through the EIP. A comprehensive enterprise search system addresses that problem. A more subtle and challenging problem is the sense that knowledge workers cannot get the real story from the portal. Sure, there may be best practices, case studies, system documentation, and project reports, but how accurate are these? Have they been sanitized so they are closer to marketing case studies than to logs of project histories and decision-making processes, complete with wrong turns, mistakes, and failures? Threaded discussions are important for collaboration during a project, but they are also valuable as records of issues confronted by teams and their solutions. The more frank the discussion of decision-making processes (e.g., "Why was component X used instead of component Y?") and mistakes along the way, the more likely we are to build trust in the EIP.

"Build it and they will come" is not a sound design strategy for EIPs. We need to know what kind of information the knowledge workers want, where it is located, and how to capture it. If users can find what they need and trust what they find, they will adopt the portal, IT will get its ROI, and the emperor will finally have something to wear.

## Lack of Sponsorship

Someone outside the portal project team needs to be excited about the portal. Ideally, both executives and users become early promoters of the project. These are the people within an organization who can draw attention to a portal, make a case for its use, and obtain the funding required to realize its potential. Executive sponsors and early adopters can also help overcome the aversion to accepting new tools and processes.

Executives must see a clear business benefit from the portal to expend time and resources on the system. At least one executive sponsor should be on board before development begins. This sponsor should secure funding for the project, articulate a clear message about the need for the portal, and resolve organizational roadblocks that limit adoption of the system.

Early adopters can effectively spread the word about the value of a portal. Of course, we secure early adopters only when the portal solves pressing business problems that are important to them. Engage potential users early in the development process so their requirements are understood. Keep close communications with them so they understand design decisions and trade-offs while the development team gathers continuous feedback on its efforts.

## Organizational Inertia and Resistance to Change

Resistance to change is probably the single most difficult problem to overcome with respect to portal adoption. While no technique will work in all cases, a combination of several approaches such as the following can lessen the problem.

- Ask an executive sponsor to mandate the use of an anchor application within the portal and eliminate alternative systems, such as client/server versions. This tactic will increase use, but often grudgingly. E-mail and time/expense tracking are good candidates.

- Provide something in the users' personal interest, such as 401K reports and vacation time request forms.
- Use document management and collaboration features of the portal as a repository for project management. Discourage the use of shared network drives for sharing content within teams and departments.
- Provide a service not available outside the portal. For instance, a single search system that indexes the portal, document management systems, shared network drives, and public e-mail folders will attract users.
- Do not try to engage all employees, customers, or partners at once. Concentrate on high-value users, secure their adoption, and expand from that base.

Technical innovation will not change attitudes or organizational inertia, but when combined with other best practices that support portal adoption, technology can help dispel concerns about the amount of work required to change.

Taken together, these methods for promoting adoption can fundamentally change the way an organization operates and shares information. The case study of CARE Canada provides a good example.

## CASE STUDY: CARE Canada's Grassroots-Driven Knowledge Management Strategy

Many of us use terms like *fire drill* and *crisis* when talking about a problem at work, but CARE Canada is in the business of responding to real crises. A nonprofit, nongovernmental agency dedicated to serving developing regions struck by natural disaster and violent conflict, CARE Canada depends on portal technology to manage information, retain organizational knowledge, and learn from past projects.

### The Problem: The Need to Rapidly Share Best Practices

The CARE Canada GYST project was driven by two strategic issues. First, the organization has to use highly repeatable processes to rapidly respond to crises like hurricanes and volcanic eruptions. These processes are documented in protocols, manuals, and other procedures. In addition, CARE Canada professionals harbor a wide range of tacit knowledge in the form of expertise and past project experience. This information is essential for site disaster relief efforts, but the organization needed a way to send that information wherever it was needed around the globe, with no time for establishing a permanent information infrastructure.

The second problem is common to virtually all enterprises: Valuable organizational experience left CARE Canada when professionals moved on. To compound the problem, CARE Canada's collective expertise is distributed over 80 countries where professionals use a range of disparate platforms. There was no single resource to which staff members could turn when responding to crises. CARE Canada collaborated with e-mail and satellite links, but these techniques lacked a historical repository. The end result was a system that created barriers to learning from past experience and no ability to detect trends across projects.

### The Solution: Gather All Project-Related Content in a Single Repository

The solution to CARE Canada's KM problem was based on a simple premise: Collect and index every piece of documentation related to projects. This included manuals, project log reports, e-mails, online discussions, memos, procedures, and policies. Open Text Livelink was chosen for the portal for several reasons. Livelink's document-centric model and support for threaded discussions met CARE Canada's initial functional requirements, and the cost of ownership, scalability, and adaptability to future change protected the investment moving into the future. Figure 4.1 shows a typical folder contain-

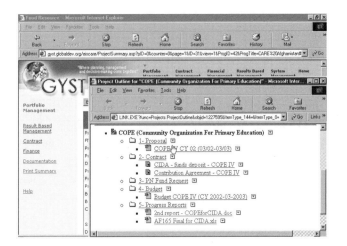

**Figure 4.1    CARE Canada's collaboration portal provides access to best practices across projects.**

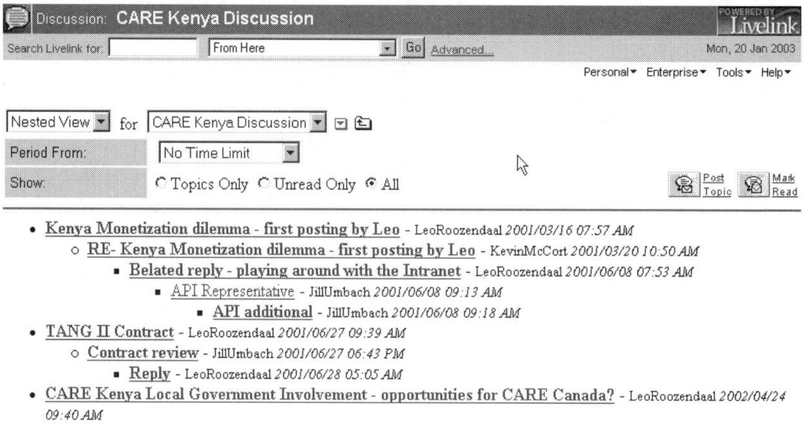

Figure 4.2     The portal also enables indexed threaded discussions.

ing documentation on the organization's repeatable processes. Figure 4.2 depicts a typical threaded discussion between staff members.

CARE Canada developed the Link system around Open Text Livelink but also included integration with Microsoft SQL Server 7, Microsoft Exchange, Microsoft Internet Information Server (IIS), and Microsoft Office applications. The system, deployed on Windows NT running on Intel platforms, uses a main server in the Canadian offices and eight remote servers across the world. Additional remote servers are added as local infrastructures can support them.

To improve the depth and quality of collaboration, CARE Canada integrated real-time video conferencing with Livelink. The organization chose the peer-to-peer solution iVisit, from Eyematics, Inc., for its resiliency and suitability for both high and low bandwidth network connections. According to Gerard van der Burg [2002], Vice President of the Global Development Group,[2] responsible for CARE Canada's IT and KM infrastructure, the distributed architecture was a key feature in the decision to use iVisit since no single bad connection would disrupt the rest of the video conference. With

---

[2] Global Development Group is a not-for-profit organization created by CARE Canada that provides IT and human resource services to CARE Canada and other not-for-profit organizations. For more information, see http://www.globaldev.org.

teams in disaster sites around the world, network reliability can never be taken for granted.

## Return on Investment

ROI is not a valid metric for CARE Canada, according to van der Burg [2002]. First, CARE Canada did not keep metrics on its processes before implementing the GYST system so the organization had no baseline for comparison. Second, CARE Canada is constantly in motion, and it's hard to measure the contributions of specific elements of the processes. Finally, even if they could formulate some measures, most executives would be skeptical of the relevancy and accuracy of those measures.

GYST has become woven into the fabric of CARE Canada operations, like phones and e-mail systems in most businesses. While it is difficult or impossible to measure ROI for these kinds of everyday tools, none of us would want to get along without them. A similar argument could be made for CARE Canada's GYST system.

## Lessons Learned

Successful KM systems tend to snowball as content is added to the system. Staff members become dependent on the system, frequently using it to find information, track old e-mails, and conduct online conferencing. This in turn fosters a culture where others adopt these habits and eventually add their own content to the system. Like the circumference of a circle, the boundaries of the KM system expand and include new areas. Eventually the growth process becomes self-sustaining.

Initiating and maintaining this type of self-sustaining process is difficult when KM systems are proscribed from the top down. KM literature is filled with discussions and advice on how to recognize and reward employees for sharing knowledge. CARE Canada has avoided the issue by building a system that fundamentally fits the way staff members work—the designers ensured a suitable fit by taking an evolutionary approach to system design and deployment. "Build it and they will come" design strategies rarely work in portal applications.

## Best Practices

CARE Canada's portal is broadly adopted because the designers and developers delivered a portal with the content users need for their most challenging work. We can see three best practices at work here.

- **Let user needs drive development and deployment.** CARE Canada provided portal solutions to small groups with a pronounced need. In turn, they used the system, pressed for specific additions to the system, and introduced the portal to others in the organization. Users in this type of grassroots approach felt more ownership of a system adapted to their needs, which in turn established the portal as a permanent and integral component of CARE Canada's ability to provide relief services around the world.
- **Index every piece of content related to collaborative efforts.** E-mails and online discussions are as important as policies and procedures when it comes to understanding the full picture of a project, how decisions were made, what options were tried, and which ones actually proved effective. Note, this "index everything" philosophy applies to collaboration, not to document creation in general. CARE Canada does not index every document on users' hard drives. Establishing appropriate boundaries that define relevant content is essential to ensure significant content is not missed and irrelevant details are not included in the KM repository.
- **Start KM initiatives around well-documented, repeatable processes.** Existing documentation provides core content, which is later augmented with e-mails, discussions, and other collaborative communications. Staff members spend less time searching for information they know exists and must be used in particular situations. That leaves them more time to respond to other, more demanding tasks. Meeting a need is a better incentive to use a KM system than is the promise of a future reward.

These best practices apply to any portal with significant amounts of unstructured content, not just KM portals.

Content used with permission of Gerard van der Burg of CARE Canada.

## Conclusion

Promoting adoption is unlike other challenges that portal developers face. Of course, technical issues come into play with adoption. If a portal is unstable or slow, few people will want to use it. However, most of the issues we confront in this arena are organizational and require a firm understanding of business needs and existing processes as well as a willingness of users to change. To ensure adoption of your portal, follow the best practices found in successful portals and outlined in this chapter.

A key point to remember is that promoting adoption is a continuous process. Keeping in close contact with users, soliciting their ideas, and meeting their needs is key to ensuring a portal becomes woven into the fabric of everyday business in your organization.

## References

Aiken, Matt, and Dan Sullivan. 2002. "Best Practices in Enterprise Information Portal Adoption: 5 Key Drivers." *DM Review*, November. Accessed in June 2003 at *http://www.dmreview.com/master.cfm?NavID=55&EdID=5963*.

Sullivan, Dan. 2002a. "Ensuring Adoption of Information Portals." *DM Review*, August. Accessed in June 2003 at *http://www.dmreview.com/master.cfm?NavID=55&EdID =5569*.

————. 2002b. "When the Emperor Has No Clothes." *DM Review*, September. Accessed in =June 2003 at *http://www.dmreview.com/master.cfm?NavID=55&EdID =5676*.

Red Hat. 2002. "Customer Profile: Siemens: ICN ShareNet." Accessed in June 2003 at *http://www.redhat.com/software/rhea/customers/siemens/*.

van der Burg, Gerard. 2002. Personal interview, April.

Wenger, Etienne. 1999. *Communities of Practice*. New York: Cambridge University Press.

# CHAPTER FIVE

# Measuring Portal Return on Investment: A Crash Course

IT practitioners well versed in software development methodologies, networking protocols, and architectural design principles are finding they need to master (or at least manage) a new domain: capital expenditure analysis. The financial management side of business is now demanding—and getting—better information on the financial impact of IT projects. In this chapter, we examine the common methods for assessing the financial aspects of portal implementations, with particular emphasis on ROI, including an example of ROI calculations. The chapter concludes with a discussion of best practices in ROI and related measures that take into account the concrete financial foundations as well as the nebulous but real nonmeasurable organizational factors that influence the overall impact a portal will have on an organization.

## The Need for Financial Impact Analysis

Ten years ago few IT managers and developers knew terms like *return on investment*, *net present value*, and *internal rate of return*, and fewer still had to work with them. Those days are gone. Several factors have permanently changed the IT landscape.

- Business is fundamentally e-business. IT is more tightly woven into the fabric of everyday and strategic business operations than it was prior to the advent of the Web. Many non-IT executives expect IT expenditures to answer to the same financial scrutiny as other capital expenditures, like manufacturing equipment.

- Well-publicized overruns and delayed implementations in enterprise resource management and customer relationship management have raised awareness of the difficulties of implementing enterprise-scale applications. Portals may be seen by some as just another hyped technology that promises more than it can deliver. Forcing IT practitioners to document assumptions about costs and benefits can help minimize any inclinations to oversell a technology.

- There is some debate about whether or not business is changing faster than in the past, but the speed of current changes and the recent weakness in the economy have forced IT departments to slow their rate of spending growth. The focus now, according to recent surveys, is on core equipment and services that offer "more direct return on investment" [McCormick 2001].

- Many technology options are available to IT executives. Which is more valuable to a business: an enterprise information portal, an outsourced backup and recovery service, or a storage area network? What if we throw in the need to conduct a full security audit, install intrusion detection systems, and revise policies and procedures related to access controls? From a technology perspective we are comparing apples and oranges. These choices need to be translated into a common form: business benefit. Business benefit is measured in dollars, and going from technologies to dollars means calculating ROI and other financial measures.

Now it is time to turn to some common techniques that will help quantify the value of a portal to your organization. Be warned, though—behind the veil of financial terminology and mathematical formulas, these calculations depend on assumptions that are often best guesses and sometimes questionable. They are helpful for comparing potential IT expenditures and forcing us to assess the impact of a portal, but they should not be given the kind of credence we give to scientific or philosophical insights. If a vendor claims its portal will save you $500,000 in the first year, nod agreeably and then start digging with the tools in the next section.

## Tools for Analyzing Capital Expenditures

No single measure is generally accepted as the best way to measure the value of an expenditure, but several are used in various combinations depending on organizations' needs. The most common measures are the following:

- Present value
- Net present value
- Payback period
- Return on investment
- Internal rate of return

Each of these is described below along with its advantages and disadvantages.

### Present Value

The amount of money available to you now is worth more than the same amount of money available to you a year from now. The reason is that you can invest that money and earn interest or increase the value of an equity. This is the basic idea behind present value. A sum of $1,000 invested today at 10% annual interest will be worth $1,100 in one year. Similarly, the value of $1,100 a year from now is equivalent to having $1,000 today, assuming a 10% rate of return.

A term frequently used in ROI calculations is **discount rate**. The discount rate is the interest rate used to determine the present value of money. For example, if we knew we would receive $1,100 one year from now and we wanted to know what that amount would be worth to us today, we would apply a discount rate, such as 10%. In that case, the present value of the $1,100 is $1,000.

From the perspective of deciding whether or not to invest in a portal, we need to understand the value of the savings we will realize over the life of the portal. First of all, let's base our calculations on a three-year time period of estimated savings accrued. This is a common assumption in IT financial assessments since it is reasonable to assume that in three years we will probably implement significant upgrades to the portal. Also, we will assume that the portal will save $100,000 per year each year for those three years. (In reality, the savings will vary by year, but we are simplifying for purposes of the example. A more realistic example appears later in the chapter.) We will continue to assume a 10% discount rate. The present value of that savings is determined by the following equation:

$$\$100,000 / (1.1) + \$100,000 / (1.1)^2 + \$100,000 / (1.1)^3 = \$248,685$$

In other words, the $300,000 savings we will realize over the next three years with the portal is equivalent to having $248,685 in hand today. This principle of measuring the present value of future savings is essential to most methods for measuring the value of capital expenditures.

Here is the general formula for three-year investments:

Amount Saved 1st Year / (1 + Discount Rate) + Amount Saved 2nd Year / (1 + Discount Rate)$^2$ + Amount Saved 3rd Year / (1 + Discount Rate)$^3$

We will use this formula in another commonly cited measure, net present value.

### Net Present Value

The net present value (NPV) of an investment takes into account the fact that savings occur over time and require an initial investment. The NPV is the present value of each year's savings minus the initial costs. Continuing with our example above, let's assume the initial cost of the portal was $200,000. The NPV of the portal investment is determined by this equation:

$100,000 / (1.1) + $100,000 / (1.1)$^2$ + $100,000 / (1.1)$^3$ − $200,000 = $48,685

Here is the general NPV formula for three-year investments:

Amount Saved 1st Year / (1 + Discount Rate) +
Amount Saved 2nd Year / (1 + Discount Rate)$^2$ +
Amount Saved 3rd Year / (1 + Discount Rate)$^3$ − Initial Costs

Recurring costs, such as software maintenance fees, should be accounted for in the amount saved each year:

Amount Saved Nth Year = Total Savings Nth Year −
Recurring Costs Nth Year

The benefit of NPV is that it provides a measure of the value of the investment in today's dollars. It does not tell us when we will realize that savings, so for that we turn to calculating the payback period.

### Payback Period

The payback period is the amount of time before the cost of the portal is paid for by its savings. The calculation is simple—divide the initial costs by the annual (or monthly) savings.

For example, a $200,000 portal that realizes $100,000 in annual savings has a payback period of two years.

Payback Period = $200,000 / $100,000 per year = 2 years

This measure quickly tells us how long it will take to recoup the initial investment, but it does not take into account the present value of the investment. This is especially problematic when the payback periods are long, for example, greater than three years. Here is the present value of saving $100,000 at 10% annual interest over the course of five years.

| Year | Savings | Present Value |
|------|---------|---------------|
| 1 | $100,000 | $90,909 |
| 2 | $100,000 | $82,645 |
| 3 | $100,000 | $75,131 |
| 4 | $100,000 | $68,301 |
| 5 | $100,000 | $62,092 |

The present value of the savings in year 5 is only $62,092—less than two-thirds of the nominal dollar amount we expect to save. Payback periods are best used for short periods and should always be used in conjunction with other measures such as NPV and ROI.

## Return on Investment

ROI is the most commonly discussed financial measure in IT. It has many advantages over the other measures. It is well known, it takes into account total cost and total benefit, and it is expressed as a percentage so it is easy to compare with other investment options.

ROI is calculated as the present value of future savings and increased income divided by the initial costs.

Again, you need to account for recurring costs in future years. For purposes of this formula, net benefit is defined as:

Net Benefit = Savings + Increased Revenue – Recurring Costs

Here's the basic three-year formula for ROI:

[1st Year Net Benefit / (1 + Discount Rate) +
2nd Year Net Benefit / (1 + Discount Rate)$^2$ +
3rd Year Net Benefit / (1 + Discount Rate)$^3$] / Initial Cost

Now we will make our example slightly more complicated. Instead of a simple $100,000 a year savings, let's assume the portal has the following savings and impacts on sales over the next three years.

| Year | Savings | Increased Revenue | Recurring Cost | Net Benefit |
|------|---------|-------------------|----------------|-------------|
| 1 | $75,000 | $10,000 | – | $85,000 |
| 2 | $65,000 | $30,000 | $25,000 | $70,000 |
| 3 | $100,000 | $50,000 | $25,000 | $125,000 |

Continuing to assume the initial cost is $200,000, the ROI for this investment is calculated as follows:

($85,000 / (1.1) + $70,000 / (1.1)$^2$ + $125,000 / (1.1)$^3$) / $200,000 = 115%

ROI is often used with NPV to get both a sense of the rate of return and the magnitude of the benefit.

## Internal Rate of Return

One more calculation, the internal rate of return (IRR), is sometimes used on large capital expenditures. It is more complex than the other calculations but similar to ROI. IRR is used to compare alternative investment options, such as deploying a portal versus installing a storage area network. The basic question answered by IRR is, given the net benefit of an investment spread over time, at what discount rate does the present value equal zero? Since we're driving the present value of the investment to zero, we can compare two or more investments on an equal basis; the one with the highest rate is the best investment.

Calculating IRR requires an iterative process that starts with a reasonable guess. Microsoft Excel's XIRR function and the Star Office IRR function can be used for these calculations. The IRR for the previous example is about 17.53% because

$$\$85,000 \text{ / } (1.1753) + \$70,000 \text{ / } (1.1753)^2 +$$
$$\$125,000 \text{ / } (1.1753)^3 - \$200,000$$

is approximately 0. (Actually, it is −7, but this is close enough for our purposes.)

IRR is often used with NPV since they complement each other in a number of ways [Martin 1997]. While the NPV calculation is sensitive to the selected discount rate, IRR calculates a discount rate based on an objective criteria, that is, driving the present value to zero. IRR is a percentage, not an absolute amount, so dissimilar projects can be compared along with projects that have different time periods.

In practice, a combination of ROI and NPV are usually used to measure the value of portals. When choosing between two or more projects, IRR is also frequently used.

## Now the Hard Part . . .

These formulas are straightforward, but they hide the single biggest problem with these types of calculations—how do you estimate savings and increased revenues? We can estimate that a business user will save one hour per week looking for information by using a portal-provided search engine. Will such 12-minute-per-day savings actually impact the bottom line, perhaps through increased productivity? If not, should these figures be included in the final ROI calculation? When the number of users is small, this type of factor will have little influence on the ROI; however, when we multiply the single-person savings by thousands of users, the effect becomes significant. The question of what to include and what not to include in ROI calculations is the root of most disagreements about ROI. Frequently, multiple scenarios with different assumptions are used to develop a better understanding of the range of possible benefits.

In addition, we should always develop several scenarios to understand how sensitive these calculations are to changes in our assumptions. For example, if our estimated benefits were 10% less than expected each year (not an unreasonable assumption, especially when looking so far out into the future), the ROI for our hypothetical portal would be closer to 104%. In some cases, this will not change the decision to deploy a portal. Other situations are not so clear cut; if another project has an ROI of 108% and an attractive payback period, which should be funded? The IRR could be the tie breaker, but even that depends on the net benefit so it too is influenced by our assumptions. In close situations like this, it is essential to understand where your estimates come from, how valid they are, and how much margin of error they might entail.

Finally, as we use these calculations we should remember that none of them account for risk. There is the risk that the project will fail or, more likely, be a partial success. There is the risk that our assumptions will be proven incorrect. For example, the rate of ROI could change if the economy slows or inflation picks up. There is also the risk that our estimates about benefits will not be realized even if the project is a success and external factors (e.g., the economy) do not undermine our assumptions. We need to remember that even if we all agree on the perfect ROI and NPV measure, risk factors outside our control can easily change the outcome.

## Calculating a Portal ROI and Related Measures

Now that we have ways to calculate ROI and related measures, we can turn our attention to the time-consuming and usually controversial part of the exercise: estimating the net benefit. The net benefit is composed of basically three parts: total savings, additional revenues, and total costs. We usually measure these for one-year periods. Let's examine each of these in more detail.

### Identifying Total Savings

Portals save money for organizations because portals decrease the cost of distributing and finding information, decrease development and deployment costs, and improve self-service operations. Some of the more specific ways portals lead to savings include the following:

- Reduced printing and distribution costs
- Reduced telecommunications costs, such as long distance and fax charges
- Decreased time required to find information
- More frequent access to detailed operational information, leading to better decision making
- Better forecasting with detailed information, leading to more efficient operations
- Faster identification of unprofitable sales lines or relationships
- Lower training costs with a single point of access to information
- Ability to scale operations without an equivalent increase in labor costs

- Reduced IT support costs due to self-service and online help
- Reduced data duplication (e.g., fewer large files attached to e-mail messages sent to multiple mailing lists)
- Reduced cost of e-business application deployment
- Reduced travel expenses
- Reduced costs due to redeployed hardware
- Reduced call center and other support costs due to partner and employee self-service

Savings are generally broken into two groups: hard savings and soft savings. Hard savings are easily quantified with agreed-upon numbers. Printing, distribution, and telecommunication charges are hard savings. Hard savings also include reduced spending in infrastructure costs. For example, a multitude of departmental and regional Web servers can be redeployed to other uses when the firm consolidates employee information in a single portal repository.

Soft savings, on the other hand, are harder to quantify because they are not easily separated out as distinct line items. Improvements in employee productivity, reduced help desk costs with self-service applications, and better forecasting leading to improved operations are all examples of soft savings. These soft savings also fluctuate and have some element of random chance. For example, with more timely and detailed reports, a line-of-business manager might identify an unprofitable line of services in a particular region that was previously unnoticed because the problem was masked when aggregated with other profitable lines. How can we account for this in an ROI estimate? Should we assume we have unprofitable segments of business? If so, how much are they costing us, and how long will it be before we find them? Clearly, these cases do occur. Better reporting helps identify them, but we cannot predict them with any certainty and should not assume them in ROI calculations. Instead, we should concentrate on soft savings that have some level of predictability.

Predictable soft savings include reduced training time and reduced numbers of calls to help desks and human resource (HR) departments due to self-service portals. Savings can be estimated based on the cost per response in the help desk or HR department. For example, if the total cost of responding to a help desk call is $25 (calculated by dividing the total help desk cost by the number of responses per year), and you expect to reduce the number of calls by 1,000, the accounting savings is $25,000. This does not necessarily mean a reduction of $25,000 in a department's expenses; the costs are simply reassigned to other areas because help desk staff is available for other tasks. We also need to remember that some of the time saved will not be used productively. Like internal combustion engines, conversion of potential energy to work is never 100% efficient. Always use a conversion factor when estimating the impact of savings due to staff time. Conversion rates of 50% to 60% are reasonable starting points for discussion. You should vary the conversion rates in multiple ROI scenarios with lower conversion rates for conservative estimates and higher rates for best-case scenarios.

### Estimating Additional Revenues

In addition to saving companies existing and future expenditures, portals can also lead to additional revenues. Some common examples of revenue generators include the following:

- Improved customer retention through customer service portals
- Reduced time to conduct sales, allowing sales staff to increase the number of leads pursued
- Better access to information about leads, improving the conversion rate of leads to sales
- Improved sales due to sharing proposals, market data, and related information between sales territories and divisions
- Faster time-to-market for new products

Additional revenues, like savings, are hard and soft. Hard revenues can be directly attributed to the portal, for example, selling products through the Web to areas not served by your business's brick-and-mortar stores. Other revenue improvements are soft because they are more difficult to measure. Customer self-service can drive the entire ROI behind a portal deployment. For example, one insurance company justified a customer service portal based solely on improving the customer retention of its top clients. Again, predictability is also a factor. A telecommunications company attributes a collaboration portal with successfully winning a major contract. The sales team, with little experience in the particulars of the customer's requirements, was able to build a winning $3 million proposal around a similar proposal developed by another sales group halfway around the world [Red Hat 2002]. These types of success stories are not uncommon, but we cannot depend on them when calculating ROI.

Soft revenue enhancements are best built around estimates of improved conversion of leads to sales and more time for sales personnel to work with clients. Here again a conversion rate is required. If a sales team saves 10 hours per week looking for information, how will that affect sales? An increase of 20% in effective selling time may translate into a marginal increase of 3%, 5%, or possibly 10% depending on other factors, such as market size, market saturation, and the ability to up-sell and cross-sell other products. Like soft savings, soft revenues are best understood through multiple scenarios ranging from worst-case to best-case options.

### Assessing Total Costs

The third major element of ROI calculations is the cost. Fortunately, many of the costs associated with portal deployments are easy to identify and estimate. They include expenses for the following:

- Portal design and implementation
- Initial portal server license
- Client or per-user software license fees
- Application server
- Ongoing maintenance
- Ancillary software (e.g., single sign-on server, categorization tools, Web publishing tools)
- Network hardware
- Network monitoring and security software
- Security audit
- Additional network/telecommunication charges
- Installation consulting
- Customization consulting
- Legacy application integration consulting
- Project management overhead
- Portal administration
- User training

When estimating costs, keep several factors in mind. First, determine the level of reliability required for your application. Failover servers may be required, and that will increase the total cost of hardware as well as add to system administration overhead. Second, plan for growth, especially with high-volume, customer-facing portals. In addition to servers, you might need to purchase load-balancing hardware. Security should not take a backseat to other features, and in heavily used portals, enhanced security systems might be required. Plan for a security audit before deploying high-volume portals. Third, vendors love to tell the world about out-of-the-box, thirty-day deployments of portal applications; however, in reality, most portals will need design and implementation work, including integration with existing systems, customization, and additional tools, such as advanced search and taxonomy generation tools. Plan on using consulting services for customization and integration, at least for the first few months. Finally, users will need training. Fortunately, most users are familiar with Web browsers so you can target training to the specific features of your portal, such as finding HR information and navigating a threaded discussion.

No two ROI analyses will be identical, but the basic process is the same. In the next section we will follow the development of an ROI assessment for a sample enterprise information portal.

## Calculating ROI for a Portal

This section depicts a hypothetical enterprise information portal for internal employees and franchise partners. Here's the basic business scenario. The fictional company, Neighborhood Auto Parts, is a franchise with 50 stores in a six-state region. These stores, which provide one-stop shopping for weekend auto repair and restoration enthusiasts, stock replacement parts, tools, equipment, and specialty parts. Neighborhood Auto Parts runs regular specials and sales and must get information about these promotions to each store in a timely manner. Company managers at headquarters also generate weekly sales reports for each store, listing sales by part and vehicle type. These reports are faxed to store managers on Monday mornings. Since the company provides parts for 45 different makes and uses 35 different parts categories, the reports show only high-level aggregate numbers, such as the dollar value of batteries and related accessories for Hondas and the total number of shocks and struts for Fords sold that week. Store managers are frustrated because they have to reenter data from the faxed reports into their own spreadsheets, they can't compare their sales to those of other stores in the chain, and they do not have prior year comparisons unless the store managers track that data themselves. Internally, managers at headquarters have similar problems, but they can access a recently deployed data warehouse through a client/server ad hoc query tool.

Neighborhood Auto Parts is considering deploying a portal that would allow store managers to access the data warehouse through a Web-based ad hoc query tool. The company would provide 20 standard reports in addition to the query tool. Also, since store data would be uploaded to the Neighborhood Auto Parts data warehouse each night, store managers would have access to one-day-old instead of one-week-old data. The portal would also allow headquarters to distribute information on sales and promotions faster and less expensively through the Web. The portal product would support threaded discussions so store managers could post questions to other store managers and headquarters personnel. The company plans to post franchise information, FAQs about store procedures, and other management documentation in an effort to improve consistent customer experience across stores.

As part of the decision-making process, the company conducts an ROI analysis. Table 5.1 shows a summary of the portal's ROI.

**Table 5.1    Basic ROI Calculation for a Medium-Sized Business's Enterprise Portal**

| Item | Year 1 | Year 2 | Year 3 |
|---|---|---|---|
| **Initial Costs** | | | |
| Portal server and related hardware | $50,000 | | |
| Additional networking equipment | $25,000 | | |
| Portal licenses | $125,000 | | |
| Consulting | $100,000 | | |
| Internal deployment costs | $50,000 | | |
| Training | $25,000 | | |
| **Total Initial Costs** | **$375,000** | | |
| **Recurring Costs** | | | |
| Training | | $50,000 | $50,000 |
| Consulting | | $25,000 | $25,000 |
| Administration | $40,000 | $40,000 | $40,000 |
| Internal development | | $40,000 | $40,000 |
| Maintenance and support contracts | | $20,000 | $20,000 |
| **Total Recurring Costs** | **$40,000** | **$175,000** | **$175,000** |
| **Savings** | | | |
| Decreased printing and distribution costs | $25,000 | $25,750 | $26,523 |
| Reduced time searching for information | $108,000 | $111,240 | $114,577 |
| **Total Savings** | **$133,000** | **$136,990** | **$141,100** |

*(continued)*

**Table 5.1    Basic ROI Calculation for a Medium-Sized Business's Enterprise Portal** (*cont.*)

| Revenue Increases | | | |
|---|---|---|---|
| Improved branding with consistent operations across stores | $50,000 | $50,000 | $50,000 |
| Improved store operations due to more manager time on floor | $100,000 | $100,000 | $100,000 |
| Improved cross-selling by identifying underperforming sales | $50,000 | $50,000 | $50,000 |
| More effective advertising due to earlier information about upcoming promotions | $25,000 | $25,000 | $25,000 |
| **Total Revenue Increases** | **$225,000** | **$225,000** | **$225,000** |
| **Net Benefit** | **$318,000** | **$186,990** | **$191,100** |
| **Discount Rate** | **0.05** | **0.05** | **0.05** |
| ROI | 170%[a] | | |

[a] The 170% ROI is derived according to the ROI formula:
$[\$318,000 / 1.05 + 186,990 / (1.05)^2 + 191,100 / (1.05)^3] / \$375,000$

Estimating the initial costs is straightforward. The company would need to invest in a new server, some additional networking equipment and related software, and portal licenses just to get started. The cost of design and deployment consultants is next, followed by the cost of internal staff support. Training is the last initial cost.

Administration is considered a recurring cost because it is paid from the operating budget instead of the capital budget that would fund this portal project. The company expects to continue to train new managers on the portal and introduce new features for all managers, so it allocates $1,000 per year per manager for that training. The other recurring costs cover additional development and administration as well as portal software maintenance fees. The company estimates one half-time administrator, whose annual cost (salary plus benefits) is $80,000 per year, would manage the portal. Similarly, the company assumes one half-time developer at the same rate would continue with portal development.

Savings would result from two elements. First, the company would save on the cost of printing and faxing weekly reports. The company estimates the total labor and material cost to be $25,000 in the first year. These costs are expected to increase at a rate of 3% per year.

Second, managers would spend less time looking for information because the portal would provide online access to data. This assumes the average manager's fully loaded rate is $75,000 per year or approximately $36 per hour. If each manager in the 50 stores saved 2 hours per week, that would result in a gross savings of $3,600 per week or $180,000 per year (assuming 50 working weeks and two weeks of vacation per manager per year). Since this is a labor savings we use a conversion factor of 0.6 to yield an effective savings of $108,000. Labor costs are expected to increase 3% in Years 2 and 3 so those savings are $111,240 and $114,577, respectively.

The increased revenues are difficult to estimate because the company has no experience with this application so conservative estimates are used. First, the company expects the portal to improve consistency of service across stores, which will improve customer loyalty among existing customers and increase market share as the company's reputation improves. Improving margins by $1,000 per year per store is a reasonable goal so this item should result in a $50,000 improvement per year. This is a guess; the actual margin could just as likely increase or decrease in future years so no inflation factor is used for Years 2 and 3. Similarly, if managers are saving time, they have more time to manage the store, identify underperforming product lines, and develop localized advertising campaigns. Again, the company chooses to be conservative here and estimates a total of $175,000 in increased revenues from these initiatives. This number is based on the effectiveness of other manager training programs and past sales campaign analysis.

Using these assumptions and the ROI formula presented earlier in the chapter, Neighborhood Auto Parts can expect a 170% return on its portal investment. In a real ROI analysis, you should consider different assumptions about savings and revenues to understand the range of possible ROI outcomes.

## Best Practices: ROI and Other Financial Impact Measures

Best practices for calculating ROI and related financial impact measures include those listed below.

- Identify a range of factors that determine the net benefit of the portal, including hard and soft estimates. Hard estimates can be quantified with clear and readily agreed-upon numbers. Factors such as printing and distribution costs and telecommunication charges are hard estimates. Soft estimates cannot be easily quantified and are strongly biased by best guesses and intuition. These include the effects of improved productivity, better decision making, and collaboration on improved sales and operations.
- Use a range of estimates such as likely, worst-case, and best-case scenarios. In likely scenarios, use only hard estimates and soft estimates that are reasonably well understood and that everyone involved would feel comfortable assuming. Stick to hard estimates in worst-case scenarios and use every estimate you can muster in best-case scenarios.
- Remember, portals are relatively new technologies, and reliable estimates of their benefits are frequently not available. Building a portal is radically different than building a factory.
- Change assumptions such as discount rates and soft estimates to determine the effect that small changes in inputs will have on the output of a calculation.
- Use a number of financial impact measures to get a good understanding of the magnitude of the investment return and the investment's relative performance compared to other measures. ROI, NPV, and IRR are often used. Payback period calculations are also helpful, but be careful with investments that are paid back over several years. Not accounting for the present value of the return in the payback period can have a major impact on measuring the true value of an investment.
- Do not get so absorbed in spreadsheets, formulas, and estimates that you lose sight of the fact that ROI is based on assumptions, such as discount rates, that often vary in accuracy.

## Conclusion

ROI and related measures are required now to justify virtually all significant IT investments, and portals are no exception. A family of calculations are available to the IT practitioner, but they are not flawless. Care and intellectual honesty are required when making assumptions about the soft benefits of portals. ROI and related measures are useful tools, but they are not infallible. However, at the end of the day, if you want to deploy a portal and you need to cost-justify it, use ROI, NPV, and possibly IRR. If you can sell the portal on gut feeling alone, fine—but going through the ROI exercise helps everyone understand both the hard and soft benefits of the portal.

## References

Martin, Ray. 1997. "Internal Rate of Return Revisited." Accessed in June 2003 at *http://members.tripod.com/~Ray_Martin/DCF/nr7aa003.html.*

McCormick, Garvin. 2001. "IT Spending Slowing, Not Stopping." *Datamation*, May 24. Accessed in June 2003 at *http://itmanagement.earthweb.com/ecom/article/0,,11952 _772981,00.html.*

Red Hat. 2002. "Customer Profile: Siemens: ICN ShareNet." Accessed in June 2003 at *http://www.redhat.com/software/rhea/customers/siemens/.*

# PART II

# The Variety of Portals

# CHAPTER SIX

# Characteristics of Effective E-Commerce Portals

During the dot-com boom, there was much talk about how the Internet was going to change business. Companies without Internet strategies were destined to become road-kill on the information superhighway. However, those days are gone. We now understand that the Internet is a tool for business and not a fundamental change of business. Enterprises must still acquire and retain customers, provide valued products and services at competitive prices, and realize profits for their shareholders. With those fundamental principles in mind, innovative organizations are developing customer portals to deliver goods, provide services, and grow their customer bases.

In this chapter we look at characteristics of successful e-commerce portals in both the business-to-business (B2B) and business-to-consumer (B2C) realms. Three case studies help demonstrate the importance of developing portals with these considerations in mind.

The common characteristics of effective e-commerce portals include those listed below:

- Customer trust
- Ease of use
- Multichannel integration
- Business practices that encourage customer retention
- Support for customer self-service

These characteristics span a range of different types of e-commerce sites: Web-only companies such as

Amazon.com (http://www.amazon.com) and eBay (http://www.ebay.com); primarily brick-and-mortar businesses such as Home Depot (http://www.homedepot.com) and Walmart (http://www.walmart.com); and service providers like the Vanguard Group (http://www.vanguard.com) and WebMD (http://www.webmd.com). Together these characteristics constitute a profile of minimum features expected by Web consumers.

## Customer Trust

Trust is the most important factor in securing a customer's business on the Web [Reichheld and Schefter 2000]. There are a number of ways to build trust.

Trust is often associated with a brand. Coke, Nike, Toyota, and IBM are brands recognized around the world. Customers are comfortable buying from the IBM online store because, well, it's IBM. Building brands is expensive and time consuming, but if your company has a recognized brand, trust is easier to build than for those businesses lacking that intangible asset.

Trust develops with transparency. Many sites, including Amazon.com and eBay have created review features to provide customer feedback. Book ratings and detailed customer assessments on Amazon.com are displayed along with publisher-provided marketing material. eBay's seller rating system gives buyers the chance to review opinions about the quality of merchandise and service from little-known vendors. Trust is built on the collective transparency of and potential peer review of every transaction on eBay. Without objectively managed customer feedback, small vendors would be strained to develop trust, and eBay would not succeed.

Trust grows with predictable service. Cost-conscious shoppers can easily compare prices on the Web, especially with portals dedicated to this service like BestBuys.com (http://www.bestbuys.com) and mySimon (http://www.mysimon.com). Cost can attract new customers, but if service expectations are not met, the chances of keeping those customers are thin.

Trust is also built on third-party relationships. Many health-oriented Web sites adopt third-party guidelines to secure a seal of approval from organizations like the Health on the Net Foundation (http://www.hon.ch) and URAC Health Website Accreditation (http://www.urac.org/). Web sites that gather customer information often describe their privacy policy and submit it for review to organizations such as TRUSTe (http://www.truste.org), which has developed a brand around privacy protection. Similarly, Verisign (http://www.verisign.com) has branded itself as the enabler of secure transactions on the Web. Sites that display logos from these recognized third parties are one step closer to building a trusting relationship with potential customers.

By using a combination of sales transparency, predictable service, and third-party relationships, even small vendors and Web-only businesses have developed levels of trust previously found only outside the e-commerce realm.

## Ease of Use

Ease of use is a central feature of portals in general, but a few techniques are commonly found in effective customer-facing portals:

- Personalization for commerce
- Intuitive navigation
- Rapid transaction execution

Each of these is discussed in the sections below.

### Personalization for Commerce

We want to be remembered where we shop. We should not have to describe our interests and tastes every time we physically visit a frequented shop, and now we expect the same of Web sites. Amazon.com has perhaps been the dominant business in shaping our expectations about personalization.

There are two types of information gathered for personalization: interests and transactions. Personalizing according to your interests is often done implicitly based on your buying patterns. Amazon.com analyzes your individual buying patterns and makes recommendations for other purchases. These recommendations can appear in sidebars as you shop for items or you can explicitly review recommendation lists and correct them for orders outside your usual areas of interest. (Anyone who has ordered books for children and found his or her interest profile shifted from areas like strategic planning and enterprise architecture toward Dr. Seuss and Harry Potter knows the problem with implicit profiling.)

Personalized customer portals remember who you are, where you want your books shipped, and how you like to pay for them. These portals support communities by allowing users to create their own recommendation lists for other shoppers, which in turn builds trust while promoting cross-selling. Amazon.com's 1-Click ordering adds a selection to your shopping basket, charges it to your default method of payment, and ships it to your default address. This is as personalized as a service can get without having the system order books for you.

Another effective ease-of-use feature is explicit personalization. This allows you to define areas of interest or have features enabled or disabled depending on your relationship to the organization. For example, as in the myHalliburton portal (see the sidebar on Halliburton later in this chapter), the B2B application provides content and utilities based on a user's responsibilities within the customer organization. Directories are typically used to manage this type of user data.

### Intuitive Navigation

Customers must be able to find what they are looking for relatively easily or they will not purchase. An estimated 30% of online retail customers leave sites before finding what they are looking for [Reichheld and Schefter 2000]. Chapter 1 describes in detail those aspects of information architecture that provide effective navigation schemes. The most important considerations for e-commerce portals are listed below.

- *Multifaceted search*: Simple keyword searching is a good start, but including other facets (or types of characteristics) about products such as price range, manufacturer, and feature set will help users find what they need more efficiently.
- *Multiple navigation hierarchies*: Taxonomies that are intuitive to one person are not necessarily intuitive to another. Including products in several places within a taxonomy will increase the chances of shoppers finding what they are looking for. PCs, for example, could be listed in both consumer electronics and office supplies sections.
- *Navigation sets*: Navigation sets are groups of pages linked together with few links outside the set. This makes it easy for shoppers to find related products without accidentally veering off into unrelated areas.
- *Immediate access to status information*: Typically a header area includes links to customer-centric information such as a shopping cart and account status. The constant immediate access to account information allows for rapid execution of transactions.

## CASE STUDY:  MusicNet Focuses on Ease of Use

MusicNet (http://www.musicnet.com) is the leading digital music service for streaming and downloading music online. The digital music provider partners with distributors, which currently include RealNetworks and AOL. RealNetworks' RealOne Music and MusicNet on AOL are digital music services that offer access to music online, as the now defunct Napster once did, but without the copyright violations. MusicNet's catalog contains offerings from major producers, such as Warner Music Group, BMG, EMI Recorded Music, Universal Music Group, and Sony Music Entertainment, as well as independent labels like Fantasy, Ritmotec, and Sanctuary. As a service and content provider, MusicNet's focuses on offering reliable, scalable access to content.

**The Problem: The Need for Rapid Access to Thousands of Artists and Their Music**

With more than 10,000 artists in its catalog, MusicNet faced a problem common with large-scale content providers: How can customers effectively search the repository? Since MusicNet provides content to a wide-ranging audience, the company needed to ensure that the search system was easy to use, scaled to meet company growth, and relevant to the customers' searches.

In the past, MusicNet used search tools provided with its relational database but found that they did not scale to meet the company's needs. Relational databases are designed for atomic transaction processing and require significant overhead to guarantee that transactions (e.g., transferring funds from a savings account to a checking account) are completed in their entirety or not at all (e.g., funds are not debited from savings without also being credited to checking). Search engines do not require these services, and the extra processing associated with transaction processing, such as managing redo logs, is just unnecessary overhead. Also, the generalized relational model is not needed in search engines that are more efficiently implemented using proprietary indexing schemes.

**The Solution: A Scalable Database and Effective Search Engine**

The company adopted a best-of-breed approach by using the Oracle database to store and manage content and metadata, while using Verity K2 software for searches. In addition, MusicNet implemented Verity K2's feature that allows searching the metadata of each entry in the catalog instead of searching the digital music itself.

MusicNet conducted an extensive evaluation of search vendors when selecting a search engine. MusicNet focused on the product's ease of use, ability to scale, and advanced functionalities as well as the vendor's market leadership. The company found that Verity K2 met its needs and requirements. Ease of use also goes hand in hand with one of MusicNet's core design principles: Keep it simple. Verity K2 software runs on Linux/Intel platforms that are easily configured in a brokered environment, allowing for incremental growth in servers. MusicNet has implemented Verity's advanced search features and is planning to implement other advanced features, such as automatic categorization and recommendations, at a later stage.

Keeping things simple, however, does not mean ignoring essential elements of design and maintenance. MusicNet was careful to address the "behind the scenes" issues of security and performance monitoring to ensure that security threats or creeping performance issues do not compromise the service.

## Best Practices

MusicNet's service model requires the company to reliably deliver large amounts of content to a broad audience of users in real time. To meet this objective MusicNet adopted the following design criteria.

- **Keep the architecture simple.** The network design is no more complex than it needs to be. The search system uses a brokered architecture that is scalable and manageable.
- **Start with basic features first, and add other advanced features later.** MusicNet focused on core search services at first but selected a tool that supports automatic categorization, taxonomy development, and recommendations based on past behavior. By keeping an eye on long-term enhancements as well as the immediate requirements, MusicNet is positioned to enhance its search services without changing the underlying infrastructure.
- **Turn to experts when needed.** MusicNet servers are serving content through the Internet and are therefore exposed to constant security threats. The service provider used consultants with expertise in application server security and network infrastructure security to analyze and enhance its systems and operations.

- **Monitor, monitor, monitor.** MusicNet built monitoring functions into its applications to allow it to measure performance, better understand the operations, and address performance issues effectively.

These practices enable MusicNet to deliver services to its customers today as well as to grow to meet future demand.

Information used with permission of MusicNet.

### Rapid Transaction Execution

Another characteristic of successful e-commerce sites is rapid transaction execution. Amazon.com's 1-Click, mentioned earlier, is as an example. The general principle is that a minimal number of steps should be required to finish a sale. The suggestions below will help you realize this goal.

- Provide rapid access to customer account information.
- Allow users to choose from multiple predefined payment methods; do not keep track of just one.
- Ensure that Return to Shopping links from shopping cart or account information pages return the shopper to the last navigation set visited (e.g., camping equipment) and not to the site's home page. That is like putting a shopper at the main entrance to the store after looking through his or her shopping basket.
- Track user focus. For example, Advanced Auto Parts (http://www. advancedautoparts.com) keeps information about a customer's vehicle so that when the shopper looks for a specific part, only parts for that vehicle are displayed.

Ease-of-use features are most apparent when they are absent. Personalization, intuitive navigation, and rapid transaction execution are three methods for helping your customers find and purchase what they need before they join that 30% of users who give up on sites before they can get what they came for.

## Multichannel Integration

Sales channels are proliferating. Brick-and-mortar stores, online stores, call centers, sales partners, and agents are all used in varying combinations to reach customers. For businesses, the goal is to leverage the advantages of each channel while still presenting a unified view to customers. Call centers, for example, offer personalized service to customers but cost more to operate than Web-based services. Customers want the convenience of ordering online, but they also want the ease of returning a product to the store in town rather than shipping it back. Meeting these expectations requires multichannel integration.

As we saw in the case study of Empire Blue Cross Blue Shield (Chapter 3) and as shown in this chapter's case study of the Institute for Healthcare Improvement, multichannel integration is a significant undertaking that requires enterprise application integration systems. It also requires changes in business operations. For example, commission plans may need to change so sales agents direct customers to the most convenient or cost-effective channel instead of the most lucrative venue for their commission. Merging channels is another change that can tap the advantages of each channel. Lands End (http://www.landsend.com) offers the option of speaking with a call center agent while browsing the online store. It is also imperative to provide a single, accurate view of the customer's account regardless of how many different channels the customer uses. As the Institute for Healthcare Improvement found, customers do not want to have to provide personal information at a Web site after faxing that same information for a course registration. From an IT perspective the costs and complexity of multichannel integration may not appear worth the effort, but creating a positive customer experience is essential to retaining customers [Reichheld and Schefter 2000].

## CASE STUDY:  Multichannel Integration at the Institute for Healthcare Improvement

The Institute for Healthcare Improvement (IHI, http://www.ihi.org) is a not-for-profit organization striving to improve the quality and value of health care. IHI realizes this challenging objective by targeting a range of specific needs, from improving critical care and flow through acute care to improving outcomes and reducing costs in cardiac surgery and asthma treatment. Its target customers are geographically dispersed and operationally varied. The organization reaches thousands of customers through training programs, collaborative projects, and conferences that draw attendees from around the world. It also provides multiple channels to serve its clients, including phone, fax, and Web-based registration and product sales.

### The Problem: Integrating Multiple Channels for Customer Service

The multiple channel model has served IHI's customers well but has also led to application integration challenges, the most salient of which are listed below.

- Different channels are supported by different applications. This is due in part to the fact that the IHI e-commerce site is hosted at a third-party site and cannot directly interface with the CRM system at IHI headquarters.
- Many details of IHI's integration plan have to be negotiated with its hosting provider. Exchanging data between databases can cause spikes in throughput on a network and ASP, and the Internet services provider is understandably concerned about managing those peak demand periods.
- Customer information is duplicated across multiple systems. It is not uncommon for customers to register for a course over the Web and then fax in a registration to "make sure it arrives."
- Duplicated information is difficult to detect because of variations in names and abbreviations (e.g., "J. Smith" and "John Smith"; "1 Main Street" and "One Main Street").

IHI believed it needed a consolidated view of its customers and its transactions, regardless of how these were initiated with the company. IHI quickly realized that its in-house extraction, transformation, and load (ETL) tool—Microsoft Data Transformation Services (DTS)—was not enough on its own, at least as it is typically used in data warehouse environments. On the other hand, conventional EAI tools provided functionality the company did not need, such as real-time messaging, and added complexity the company did not want. IHI instead chose to develop a custom solution combining DTS as a backbone framework for ETL services, a centralized database for metadata management, and a library of data manipulation services.

**The Solution: Enterprise Application Integration**

IHI's first pass at a custom EAI solution depended on peer-to-peer communications between applications using ETL plans in DTS. Lead designer Andy Hackbarth [2003] concluded "1) a peer-to-peer adapter model would be untenable for more than a few node systems, and 2) DTS was really not flexible or powerful enough a tool for what [IHI] was trying to do." Hackbarth realized that a centralized database with generalized representations for key entities (e.g., customers, organizations, transactions, and so on) and metadata about the data integration process would solve the company's problems.

Microsoft DTS provided the necessary tools to migrate data, but many of the operations in the data exchange required complex business logic that could not be performed using only predefined DTS components. For example, a customer added to the CRM system should be added to the Web database only if the customer has a valid e-mail address and has had valid sales transactions with IHI. When customers are added to the Web database, a temporary username and password is generated and the customer is notified by e-mail of his or her new Web account with IHI.

Another chronic challenge common to any organization that manages customer lists is the removal of duplicate names. This requires business logic sophisticated enough to identify true duplicates without mistakenly removing a nonduplicated customer. Peer-to-peer comparisons of databases for duplicates are inefficient; IHI wanted to execute the process once, comparing all customer records. Using a centralized database was the most effective solution to these business logic problems.

Hackbarth designed a hub-and-spoke model using SQL Server and DTS with the following components.

- *Central database:* This instance of SQL Server is located at IHI headquarters in Boston, Massachusetts. It stores all information gathered at the various node systems (e.g., CRM tool, Web site, and so on) in a standardized format. In contrast to the EAI tools, however, this database actually stores all the data, rather than reading it in, transforming it, and passing it along to other systems. Auxiliary uses of this database include acting as a marketing tool and as an operational data store to source a data warehouse. This database also provides a custom logging apparatus that is able to receive and store log messages from any DTS package. Although a centralized database can become a bottleneck in high-volume environments, this is not the case at IHI.
- *Data exchange DTS packages:* These are the ETL scripts between each node system and the central database. One set of DTS packages manages data flows into the central database, the other set manages outflows to node systems.
- *Business logic DTS packages:* These packages handle the manipulation of data within the central database (e.g., things like duplicate search and resolution, error logging, and so on).
- *Business logic stored procedures:* This is a library of stored procedures and user-defined functions in SQL Server that are called by the appropriate DTS packages to perform common operations across DTS packages such as adding a customer, transaction, or organization to the central database; writing a log message; searching for duplicates; and so on.

The central database was designed with several principles in mind. First, entities were modeled to include all attributes found in the node systems.

Realizing that these systems will change, IHI added the ability to represent attributes without changing either the source or central database schema. Each entity has an associated table for specifying an arbitrary field name, type, and value. This allows IHI to quickly incorporate new types of information, for example, from a partner database.

Second, source systems were not changed. Metadata about data exchanges, such as links from records in the central database back to source records in the node databases, is managed in the central database. Logging and audit controls are also handled by the central database.

Third, business logic should be reusable. Operations like adding a customer, removing a duplicate, and updating links between source and central database records are used in multiple DTS packages.

## Best Practices

IHI incorporated a number of best practices in its multichannel integration project.

- **Keep EAI as simple as possible.** The EAI system was only as complex as needed. IHI could have purchased a commercial off-the-shelf package, but most EAI packages would have introduced more complexity without significant benefits over the custom-designed solution.
- **Minimize change to source systems.** The system was designed for change but does not require modifications to source systems. A flexible, centralized database adapts to changes in business processes.
- **Address integration issues with your hosting services as soon as possible.** IHI is negotiating implementation issues with its ASP and Internet service provider. These providers are partners in core business operations, and the sooner they are brought into the design process, the better the company can prevent mistaken assumptions that can disrupt the EAI process.

Keeping the EAI architecture as simple as possible and maintaining close communications with stakeholders (e.g., hosting services) improves the chances of a successful implementation.

Information used with permission of IHI.

## Customer Retention

According to a study by Reichheld and Schefter [2000], it takes two to three years to recoup the cost of acquiring new customers. E-commerce businesses must identify profitable types of customers, attract them, and then retain them. Simply attracting visitors, counting clicks, and analyzing the most popular products is not enough.

Personalization and ease-of-use features make customers' lives easier, and communities and transparency build loyalty and trust. These are not quick fixes; they take major commitments on both the business and IT sides of an organization. As Baveja [2000] noted, "e-retailers must treat customers as assets, not transactions."

## Support for Self-Service

Customer portals are a cost-effective channel for supporting customer self-service, and they offer a number of advantages over other channels. They scale more easily than other channels and help reduce the load on those other more costly channels. One call center found that 55% of its support calls moved to the Web and wait times dropped from 12 minutes to 38 seconds when Web self-service was introduced [eGain Communications Corporation 2002]. Portals can speed responses to customers; however, organizations need to improve methods for responding to customer e-mails. In one survey, less than 25% of customer e-mails were responded to within 24 hours of receiving the inquiries [Kramer and Brendler 2001]. Effective self-service requires the following:

- Access to account information
- Access to live help when needed
- Question-answering services

Access to account information is by now standard fare. Similarly, access to live help when needed entails multichannel integration, as described earlier in this chapter. In this section, we focus on the question answering services and how they differ from traditional search tools.

Self-service is somewhat of a misnomer since the process depends critically on content management, knowledge bases, and question-answering programs. At the first level of self-service, the customer is looking for general information to solve a specific problem within his or her organization. For example, a myHalliburton user might need background material to address a problem with a poorly performing oil well; a Microsoft customer may need details on configuring a device driver. These types of questions are complex and require researching, testing, implementing possible solutions, assessing results, and sometimes beginning the troubleshooting process over again. Content management systems with well-designed facets and search systems work well in these areas.

The second level of customer service focuses on providing answers, not documents, in response to user queries. A customer question such as "Whom do I call about an error in my bill?" should not simply be answered with a list of documents that contain the words "error" and "bill." This type of customer inquiry is best responded to with an answer. The simplest approach is to use a frequently asked questions (FAQ) document. Question databases, such as Ask Jeeves (http://www.jeevessolutions.com), improve on FAQs and provide more precise answers by mapping queries to predefined questions and replying with the answers associated with those questions. Finally, more advanced natural-language-oriented search and question-answering tools, such as those from Primus Knowledge Solutions (http://www.primus.com) and Insightful (http://www.insightful.com), often provide analytic reporting on the types of questions asked, the most frequently used answers, and missing answer content.

Self-service in a portal when effectively implemented yields both cost savings and improved customer retention. As with other aspects of customer-facing portals, adopting a customer-centric design focus and understanding the user experience are essential to building a successful portal.

## CASE STUDY: Reducing Costs and Improving Customer Retention at Halliburton

Halliburton (http://www.halliburton.com) is one of the world's largest providers of products and services to the oil and gas industry. The company's offerings span the full lifecycle of oil and gas production from exploration and development through drilling and well completions to operations and maintenance.

### The Problem: Large, Geographically Dispersed Customers with Specialized Needs

With employees in over 100 countries and customers around the globe, Halliburton developed a customer portal, called myHalliburton, to improve information sharing and make it easier for customers to deal with the firm.

## The Solution: A Single Point of Access to Project Information

The portal, shown in Figure 6.1, provides a single point of access to a range of technical and administrative information. It has driven down Halliburton's costs while improving its customer operations, which in turn improve customer retention.

Technical offerings include specialized analytic tools such as simulators, best practices documentation, and private collaboration tools for communities of practice. myHalliburton also provides an expert directory so customers can quickly identify and reach Halliburton employees with specialized skills and knowledge. The commercial support features facilitate access to administrative information about a project including invoices, master contracts, field tickets, job schedules, and so on. Providing customers with full and accurate pictures of their accounts (the Plumtree portal is integrated with Halliburton's enterprise resource planning system) has not only eased customers' interactions with the company but also reduced the time required to resolve billing disputes.

Personalization features are well developed in myHalliburton. Technical services are provided based on the user's area of interest; for example, geo-

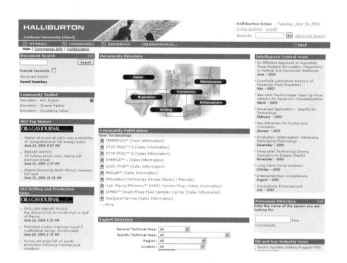

**Figure 6.1**     The myHalliburton portal provides customers with personalized access to technical and commercial information.

physicists have access to different tools than well completions engineers do. Users can customize these interests directly. Roles also determine access to collaboration forums. Users are provided commercial information only about their own projects and corporate accounts, thus ensuring the privacy of other customers. The personalization information, combined with usage patterns, also provides sales teams with more in-depth knowledge of customers and supports their efforts to tailor offerings to each customer's particular interests.

The array of features in myHalliburton is extensive, but what is the impact on the bottom line? As with most portal implementations, there are quantifiable benefits and softer, nonquantifiable benefits. The quantifiable benefits include those listed below.

- *Reducing the time required to resolve payment disputes:* Using the portal rather than mail to deliver invoices and related documentation during dispute resolution saves an average of six days per dispute. Each day of reduction in this average is worth $1.95 million per year to the company.
- *Improving sales:* In customer surveys, 40% of respondents stated that they were influenced in their decision to purchase from Halliburton because of the portal; 59% said the portal is likely or very likely to influence future decisions; and 69% left with a more positive impression of the company than they had previously held. In one year, myHalliburton influenced $53 million in business.

It is more difficult to measure the direct impact of some services (such as the technical tool suites, expert directories, and the communities of practice), but they likely contribute positively to influencing sales decisions.

The tangible and measurable improvements realized with the deployment of myHalliburton are the product of management as well as technical decisions. The overall responsibility for the portal rested with a business program manager, not in the IT department. This program manager also used the Microsoft Solutions Framework (MSF) to manage the development and deployment of the portal.[1] This methodology includes models for developing

---

[1] Information on the MSF can be found at http://www.microsoft.com/technet/treeview/default .asp?url=/technet/itsolutions/tandp/innsol/default.asp.

teams, managing iterative development and deployment processes, managing risk, and assessing readiness.

**Best Practices**

Halliburton used a number of best practices in this project.

- **Keep the focus on the customer.** The portal was designed with the customer's technical and administrative needs in mind.
- **Align the portal with the needs of the sales force.** Valuable information about customer interests can be derived from explicitly defined personalization information as well as from application and Web server logs.
- **Use conservative ROI measures.** Halliburton's program manager was careful not to overstate the impact of the portal by using identifiable and concrete savings, such as mailing time.
- **Measure the value of the portal to the customer as well as to internal operations.** By making it easier to work with Halliburton, the portal encourages customers to continue to purchase Halliburton products and services.
- **Use an iterative development methodology to deliver incremental improvements.** Iterative methodologies reduce risk and improve alignment of applications with customer needs.

Halliburton met the needs of its customers and its ROI expectations by measuring performance and aligning the portal design to well-understood requirements.

Information used with permission of Halliburton.

## Conclusion

Portals are a new channel for acquiring, serving, and retaining customers. With the acquisition costs of new customers requiring two- to three-year payback periods, it is essential to retain profitable customers. E-commerce sites that are easy to use, provide intuitive search and navigation, and rapidly complete transactions are more likely to retain customers than those that make shopping a chore. Self-service can also improve customer satisfaction (as the myHalliburton case study clearly demonstrated), and it can also drive down the cost of customer support. Portal technologies integrated with other sale and support channels deliver positive returns on investments and improve sales.

## References

Baveja, Sarabjit Singh. 2000. "Making the Most of Customers." *The Industry Standard*, March 6. Accessed in June 2003 at *http://www.thestandard.com/article/0,1902,11978,00.html.*

eGain Communications Corporation. 2002. "Case Study: Quick & Reilly and eGain." Accessed in February 2003 at *http://www.egain.com/.*

Hackbarth, Andy. 2003. Personal interview, February.

Kramer, David Ben-Gal, and Bill Brendler. 2001. "Sticky Conversations in Customer Care." *Intelligent Enterprise*, January 30. Accessed in June 2003 at *http://www.intelligentcrm.com/feature/010130/featJan1.shtml.*

Reichheld, Fredrick F., and Phil Schefter. 2000. "E-loyalty: Your Secret Weapon on the Web." *Harvard Business Review,* July–August. Accessed in June 2003 at *http://harvardbusinessonline.hbsp.harvard.edu/b01/en/common/item_detail.jhtml?id=5181.*

# CHAPTER SEVEN

# Delivering Business Intelligence and Analytics on Demand

As we saw in Chapter 6, a portal is a powerful tool for communicating with customers and allowing them to better manage their interactions with an organization. In this chapter, we turn to primarily internal users with broad needs for management information as well as specialized expertise within an organization.

Business intelligence is the practice of analyzing operational information to measure, analyze, and control production, sales, marketing, finance, and other key sectors of the enterprise. These operations and their related tools have had names like *decision support*, *executive information systems*, and *data warehouses*. The changing names have reflected both the scope of information included in these systems and the range of users who depend on them. In older hierarchical management models, those who made decisions were different from those who carried them out—only executives needed to know the big picture. Most organizations are now less hierarchical with more distributed decision making and line-of-business accountability. It is not just the executives at the top of the organization chart who are responsible for the success of a company. Managers and operational staff throughout the enterprise now share the burden.

The information needed to manage an organization is often spread across a diverse range of financial, production, and customer management systems. The role of business intelligence systems is to bring that information together and provide users with easy and fast access to key measures of company performance. Portals are the most effective delivery mechanism for getting this information out to the broad range of users who now depend on business intelligence to get their jobs done.

In addition to the need for information about operational performance, smaller numbers of people within the organization need access to specialized analytic services. Engineers drilling wells need specialized models to determine the optimal method for drilling in particular geological formations, pharmaceutical researchers need statistical expertise to analyze the results of assays, and financial analysts require complex econometric models to assess the impact of changes in a portfolio. These needs are fundamentally different from the historical operational data provided by business intelligence systems, but meeting these specialized requirements contributes to the operational efficiency just as filling the need for operational data does. Like business intelligence applications, these analytic services are most effectively deployed through portals.

This chapter provides an overview of data warehousing and analytic applications that support business intelligence. The design of these systems is fundamentally different from the more common transaction-oriented relational databases so we delve into some of the implementation details of data warehouses. We also examine different types of reporting models in business intelligence and then discuss the limits of these tools. Finally, we examine the role of analytic services for leveraging expert knowledge and best practices within an organization. The case study in this chapter demonstrates the need for and the effectiveness of analytic services in the pharmaceutical industry.

## Understanding Operations: Business Intelligence and Data Warehousing

Businesses, government agencies, and other organizations typically create information systems to optimize specific operations, such as accounting, CRM, and ERP. These systems are designed to allow rapid access to specific information, such as the status of an invoice, a customer record, or the inventory level of a specific component. They are not designed to provide the high-level, integrated views that decision makers need to get a pulse on the organization. For example, a financial analyst studying cash flow may need to know the average outstanding invoice by month and by sales region for the past twelve months, and a product manager will likely monitor the average daily inventory by product and warehouse.

Tracking these kinds of measures is not an essential function of the operational systems that manage details about transactions rather than aggregate measures over those transactions. These online transaction processing (OLTP) systems are also narrowly focused on a specific task, such as managing inventory. Even integrated packages, such as ERP and financial systems, are comprised of modules dedicated to specific tasks (e.g., material handling, inventory, accounts receivable, accounts payable, general ledger).

Rather than trying to fit a square peg into a round hole, database designers realized that it is best to develop separate systems for integrated, operational reporting. This awareness led to the practice of data warehousing (Figure 7.1).

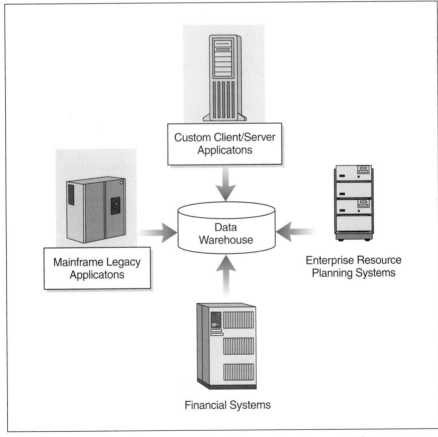

**Figure 7.1    Data warehouses combine information from multiple systems and put it into a common format to facilitate integrated, aggregate reporting.**

## Characteristics of Data Warehouses

Data warehouses have several distinguishing characteristics.

- These systems combine data from multiple sources. Operational systems such as ERP systems provide production data, financial systems supply revenue and expense data, and human resource systems present employee data.
- The data copied into a data warehouse does not change (except to correct errors). The data warehouse is a historical record of the state of an organization. The frequent changes of the source OLTP systems are reflected in the data warehouse by adding new data, not by changing existing data.
- Data warehouses are subject oriented, that is, they focus on measuring entities, such as sales, inventory, and quality. OLTP systems, by contrast, are function oriented and focus on operations such as order fulfillment.
- In data warehouses, data from distinct function-oriented systems is integrated to provide a single view of an operational entity.
- Data warehouses are designed for business users, not database programmers, so they are easy to understand and query.
- Data warehouses are designed for speed. Users interact with data warehouses—running queries, analyzing data, formulating new queries based on information gleaned from earlier queries—so the systems must be responsive.

Designers are able to implement these characteristics through a combination of database design techniques and data preprocessing.

## The Data Warehouse Environment

Data warehouses comprise a multifaceted environment that spans the information systems spectrum from operational transaction systems to systems designed for executive and front-line decision makers. There are four main elements of a data warehouse environment:

1. Source systems
2. Extraction, transformation, and load (ETL) systems
3. Data warehouse repository
4. Reporting tools and portals

Each of these is described below.

## Source Systems

As the name implies, source systems provide the raw material for the data warehouse and business intelligence systems. The design and implementation of these applications is outside the scope of the data warehouse, and source systems are typically treated as black boxes. Some of the considerations we have with regard to source systems are listed below.

- *The amount of time available to extract data from the system*: Source systems such as ERP and CRM systems have limited windows of opportunity to perform maintenance or execute long-running data extractions. Those constraints must be balanced against the need to regularly refresh the data warehouse.
- *The ability to execute incremental extractions*: Some legacy systems may not support extractions based on timestamps or other indicators of new or modified data. In these cases, the next phase (ETL) must distinguish new and modified data from existing data already in the data warehouse.
- *Multiple sources of information*: Multiple applications may maintain overlapping information, such as customer records. Prior to building the data warehouse, designers need to determine whether a particular record will be the record of source or whether partial data from multiple sources must be combined to form a record of source.

Operational systems have often evolved independently of each other. The adoption of enterprise software such as ERP and CRM systems provides the basis for consistent data sources in many organizations. However, legacy systems with inconsistent data representations are still common and need to be reconciled within the data warehouse environment. This is one of the responsibilities of ETL systems.

## Extraction, Transformation, and Load Systems

The development and management of ETL processes often require a majority of the time and resources in a data warehouse project.

The extraction process focuses on getting data out of the source systems and into a staging area for further processing. The details of this part of the operation are highly dependent on the nature of the source systems.

The transformation process uses raw data from multiple source systems, scrubbing and reformatting the data to create a consistent data set. Some of the most common operations are the following:

- Applying consistent coding schemes
- Removing duplicate records
- Reformatting text data (e.g., addresses)
- Sorting
- Calculating derived date attributes (e.g., name of the day of the week, day of the year)
- Looking up foreign key references
- Joining data streams
- Conditionally splitting data streams
- Aggregating data
- Filtering data

After applying a series of transformations, the cleansed data is loaded into the data warehouse in the final format familiar to business intelligence users.

### Data Warehouse Repository

The data warehouse repository is the long-term, historical, integrated database that supports business intelligence operations. Most are built on relational database management systems and advanced users combine them with OLAP systems as well. (See The OLAP Alternative sidebar.)

The characteristics of data warehouses were covered in an earlier section in this chapter.

## The OLAP Alternative

Before relational database systems such as Oracle and Microsoft SQL Server began including features specifically designed for dimensional modeling, a nonrelational technology, online analytic processing (OLAP), was developed to handle the aggregate analysis required in business intelligence applications.

OLAP systems use a cube model instead of relational tables for data storage. With tables, related information is separated for storage purposes and joined together at query time through identifiers known as primary keys and foreign keys. A **primary key** uniquely identifies a row in a table, for example, the "January 1, 2004" row in the time dimension could have a primary key "1895." All rows in the fact table that apply to January 1, 2004, would have a column that serves as a foreign key and holds the value

"1895." The **foreign key** is thus a reference to a primary key in another table. This design approach has many advantages, but one drawback is that even with optimizations, the process of joining tables through foreign keys can be time consuming. Cubes avoid this operation.

The cube model of storage is based on dimensions, such as time, product, region, customer, and so on. We can think of these dimensions as sides of a cube, as shown in Figure 7.2. Cubes are divided into cells; each cell corresponds to an intersection of all dimensions. For example, one cell could be defined by "January 1, 2004" (time), "myPDA" (product), and "Southwest" (region). Measures such as total units sold, cost of goods sold, total revenue, and so on are associated with cells. When users query a multidimensional cube, the OLAP system uses a series of index lookups to find a particular cell rather than executing a time-consuming join. This results in extremely fast query response times.

As we all know, there is no free lunch in information technology. The rapid response time comes at a cost of long data loads. When data is extracted from source systems and moved into an OLAP cube, the measures for a particular context are precomputed and stored in the corresponding cell (this is referred to as "rolling up" the data).

Since the star schema and the OLAP cube both use dimensional representations, it is a relatively straightforward process to integrate the two and leverage the advantages of both. Star schemas and relational databases can

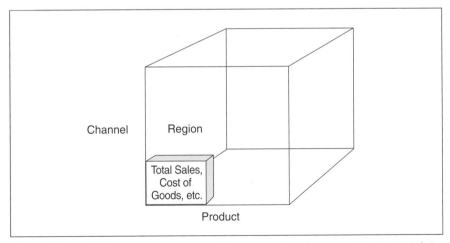

Channel     Region

Total Sales,
Cost of
Goods, etc.

Product

**Figure 7.2    OLAP systems use multidimensional cubes as a storage model.**

store enormous amounts of data in great detail while OLAP systems provide rapid access to aggregated data. OLAP query tools should be used to analyze high-level aggregates across a wide range of data, and as more details are required, users can drill down from the OLAP cube to the details stored in a star schema.

Database vendors have recognized the complementary power of OLAP and relational models and now offer embedded OLAP services within relational database engines. Both Oracle and Microsoft have taken this approach. Query and analytic tools are also becoming more integrated. For example, Oracle Express (the database vendor's OLAP tool) integrates with Oracle Discoverer (an ad hoc query tool for relational data warehouses) to provide drill-down capabilities from cubes to star schemas.

### Reporting Tools and Portals

The final piece of the data warehouse puzzle is reporting tools and often the enterprise portal. Reporting tools range from predefined reports that are generated automatically and distributed to users based on roles to advanced OLAP tools for forecasting. The most commonly used tools are the ad hoc query tool and the dashboard. Visualization tools are gaining popularity as well.

#### Ad Hoc Query Tools

These systems allow users to run parameterized reports on an as-needed basis or to create their own custom reports. At this point the ease of understanding comes into play in data warehousing. Star schemas and the ideas of context and measures are easily grasped by most users so they no longer have to depend on IT departments to generate the reports they need. Many tools even provide an additional layer of abstraction over the star schema to make the data representation closer to a business model. In Business Objects, this extra layer is called the Business Objects Universe, and in Oracle Discoverer it is aptly named the End User Layer.

Ad hoc query tools are suitable when end users have a solid understanding of the underlying business process modeled in the data warehouse and seek a detailed review of information. They should also be familiar with the key measures reported by the data warehouse and comfortable with analyzing in detail the indications of problems with a business process. For users who prefer a higher-level view of a broader spectrum of measures, use a dashboard.

*Dashboards*

Dashboards are reporting tools that display key performance indicators. These are especially useful for executives and others who need a high-level view of an organization or operation. Key performance indicators can include measures of sales pipeline, production rates, quality assurance measures, customer satisfaction indicators, revenue projections, and other information on the state of the organization.

In many organizations daily or even weekly updates of the dashboard are acceptable. Some organizations, such as retail companies, can benefit from real-time monitoring of key performance indicators. How often you should update a dashboard depends on the time required to execute a change in your organization and how frequently the source data changes. For example, online retailers can change prices immediately to adapt to changing market conditions. Information about the financial position of a company (e.g., the status of accounts payable and accounts receivable) does not generally change more frequently than once a day.

*Visualization Tools*

Visualization tools combine the best of both ad hoc query tools and dashboards. Like dashboards, visualization tools can simultaneously provide a high-level view of several measures. Like ad hoc query tools, they allow users to drill into the detail of underlying information.

When deploying business intelligence applications, use visualization tools liberally. There are several reasons for this. Visualization tools are suitable for both analytic and nonanalytic users. Also, they can convey information more rapidly than table-based reports. Designers can create visualization metaphors, like maps, that closely align to the way users think about the distribution of data. A color-coded map of a sales region, for example, can help sales managers spot trends across territories more effectively than if they had to cull the information from a tabular report.

*Portals*

Combined with ad hoc query tools, dashboards, and visualization tools, a portal can provide the flexible access to data warehouses needed by executives and line-of-business managers throughout an organization.

Portals are ideal delivery vehicles for business intelligence reporting. Portals provide single sign-on and other infrastructure support, which eases the data warehouse developer's job. Portals are easily customized to provide quick access to frequently used reports, offer a convenient place to post notices, and deliver newly generated reports. Also, remember that numbers never tell the whole story. For example, an analyst may find a problem with sales or production based on a data warehouse report. These reports do not indicate *why* a problem occurred. A portal can house several different analytic tools (e.g., forecasting and modeling tools that use historical data from the data warehouse as the basis for projections and complement the historical look provided by ad hoc query tools). Thus other tools in the portal, such as enterprise search and document management systems (see Chapter 8), can help the analyst identify the root cause of the problem.

### The Limits of Data Warehouse Reporting

Data warehousing, the workhorse of business intelligence, meets many business requirements but is not a panacea. Several factors limit the extent to which data warehousing can meet all business intelligence needs.

Data warehouses aggregate data for performance reasons. Data warehouses, unless they maintain transaction-level detail, are not appropriate sources of information for data mining, statistical analysis, and other advanced operations. Operational data stores and transaction processing systems are generally better sources of data for these applications.

Data warehouse reports can indicate problems but rarely provide all the details about anomalous measures. The trend toward integrating business intelligence and knowledge management is addressing this problem, but there is still much work to be done [Sullivan 2001; Code et al. 2002]. (See Chapter 8 for more on knowledge management.)

Data warehousing also uses a general model for analyzing operations, but in some cases specialized information and techniques are required. Fortunately, portals again lend themselves as the vehicle for choice for deploying specialized analytic services.

## Facilitating Operations: Analytic Services

Portals lend themselves to a variety of techniques for sharing information and knowledge. Data warehouses are the foundation for historical operational information; document management and collaboration tools support knowledge management practices, and specialized analytic applications provide domain-specific functions.

Analytic services can span a wide range of topics and typically have small user bases, especially compared with data warehouse users. Examples include modeling programs used by geologists in the oil and gas industry, statistical analysis programs used by pharmaceutical researchers analyzing the results of preclinical tests, financial modeling programs used by actuaries, signal modeling programs used by electrical engineers, and fraud detection analysis used by data miners in financial services industries. Understanding each of these domains requires specialized knowledge not broadly available. Analytic services allow businesses to codify some techniques and make them available to a wider audience than can be served by individual analysts alone.

The keys to successful analytic services are fourfold.

1. They should support an analyst in narrow elements of technical decision making. Analytic services cannot design a circuit, determine the efficacy of a new drug, or determine the best method to drill a well. Attempts have been made to develop expert systems that can completely solve high-valued, complex problems, but these applications are most effective when designed to support, not supplant, human experts.

2. Designers should focus on developing analytic services that address routine or computationally complex operations, that is, the "low-hanging fruit." Modeling techniques can embody the best practices of experts for solving particular problems, such as dependably identifying promising test results in drug research. (See the case study on Merck Research Laboratories.)

3. Analytic services should be deployed in a role-based framework. Suites of tools should be designed for specific user groups and rolled out incrementally.

4. End users' feedback should help shape the deployment, interface, and functionality of analytic services. No one knows the end users' needs better than they do.

Analytic services naturally complement the data-retrieval-oriented operations of data warehouses.

## CASE STUDY:  Web-Based Analytics at Merck Research Laboratories

**Drug discovery is a time-consuming and capital-intensive endeavor, on average taking 10 years and costing $800 million per drug. An early phase of drug discovery, the basic research and preclinical studies, involves testing and analyzing the ability of one chemical agent to effect change in another,**

such as a protein or enzyme. Advances in biological and chemical analytics, such as High Throughput Screening (HTS), have increased the number of tests performed from tens per day to thousands.

## The Problem: Increasing Demand for Analytic Expertise

At Merck Research Laboratories (MRL), analyzing the growing body of data generated from these tests was becoming a bottleneck in drug research. Statisticians with the expertise to assess the data could not keep up using traditional one-on-one consulting methods with scientists. To keep pace with the highly automated data generation, MRL turned to Web-based analytics to leverage its in-house expertise through the HTS StatServer project.

The goal of the project was to deliver to nonexperts the statistical tools that could help researchers identify a relatively small set of promising agents worthy of further investigation. This is done by applying statistical methods to analyze data to better understand patterns of interaction among the chemical agents and biological targets. These interactions are never identical across tests in practice. Differences in test procedures, chemicals, and a host of other factors introduce variations in results. Some variations are relatively insignificant while others are not; determining which is which is not always obvious. Statisticians have developed a wealth of techniques for dealing with variations and assessing what types of information can be reliably derived from data sets such as those derived from HTS. Unfortunately, specialized training is often required to understand these methods and to apply them appropriately.

For example, consider the common problem of false positives (test results of drugs that appear to have potency but do not) and false negatives (test results of drugs that appear to have no interactions when in fact they do). Minimizing both types of spurious results is essential to producing a manageable number of promising agents for further research. This is complicated by the fact that there is typically an inverse relationship between false positives and false negatives; that is, isolated minimization of one inflates the other. This type of task is familiar for statisticians but in high demand by scientists and so is an obvious candidate for automation.

## The Solution: Portal-Based Data Analysis Tools

To meet the needs of researchers, MRL statisticians had several requirements outside the purely statistical issues. First, they needed to work closely with HTS scientists to understand their needs. Second, the solution had to scale to accommodate dozens of potential users in North American and European research centers. Third, the solution had to be Web-based. The development team could not support a desktop-based application and all its administrative overhead. Centralization was essential.

MRL chose Insightful StatServer for both its statistical analysis features and its Web-based architecture. Using S-PLUS, StatServer's development language and environment, the development team was able to rapidly prototype and iteratively refine applications with scientists. It also provided visualization tools essential to this type of work. According to Bill Pikounis, Ph.D., of the Biometrics Research Department at MRL, "Informative and relevant visualization tools ensure effective study, interpretation, and communication of results among colleagues" [Pikounis 2002]. StatServer is a centralized statistics server with tight Web integration that makes enterprise-wide deployment much easier than with client/server applications.

The benefits to MRL are clear. A relatively small group of statisticians are now able to support a larger base of scientists, routine analysis is performed automatically so experts are free to tackle more challenging problems, and users have faster turn-around time on critical path operations. Since this initial project, the company has built a handful of other StatServer-based tools for scientists to address the wide diversity of preclinical research data analysis needs, including gene expression and traditional comparative experiments for animal pharmacology.

## Best Practices

MRL employed several best practices in this deployment.

- **Deliver analytic services with broad appeal.** MRL develops drugs to treat a wide variety of diseases, including cholesterol, inflammation, asthma, hypertension, HIV/AIDS, and osteoporosis. The development team did not focus on a single drug or disease but on a fundamental process at the core of the company's business.
- **Carefully choose the analytic techniques to deploy.** The algorithms had to produce reliable information across a wide range of data sets. Users were not in a position to determine the appropriate application of a large variety of statistical methods—they needed a toolbox of techniques that did not require specialized knowledge.

- **Work closely with the end users to refine the application.** Simply analyzing data and producing a database of results was not enough. Scientists needed visualization tools to gain insight into the results and to communicate those results to their peers.

It is worth noting that MRL did not perform an ROI analysis. The ability to reach a large number of users with an innovative system that could also provide metrics on use appealed to management without the need for a formal ROI analysis.

Content used with permission of Merck and Company.

## Conclusion

Management styles and organizational structures have changed radically over the past two decades. Gone are the days when a few executives and managers made all the operational decisions. The decentralization of decision making is driving the need for operational and management information throughout organizations, and portals are the delivery vehicle of choice for many business intelligence systems. Successful business intelligence systems share a number of common features. They are fast and easy to understand, which usually means they are designed based on dimensional models. Terms and measures are used consistently throughout the organization, which implies conformed dimensions and conformed facts. Of course, not all operational decisions are based on historical data. Analytic services provide specialized functions to small groups of users. Again, the portal framework provides the best platform for deploying suites of specialized tools to targeted users throughout the organization. In the next chapter, we will continue the discussion of information needs for internal operations but will shift our focus from structured analytics to problems in knowledge management and unstructured data management.

## References

Code, W. F., J. T. Kruelen, V. Krishna, and W. S. Spangler. 2002. "The Integration of Business Intelligence and Knowledge Management." *IBM Systems Journal* 41(4). Accessed in June 2003 at *http://www.almaden.ibm.com/software/km/bi/BIKM.pdf.*
Pikounis, Bill. 2002. Personal interview, May 31.
Sullivan, Dan. 2001. *Document Warehousing and Text Mining.* New York: Wiley.

# CHAPTER EIGHT

# Effective Knowledge Management Techniques

Many organizations today are valued as much for their intellectual assets as their physical resources. Pharmaceutical, financial services, defense, and other research-intensive enterprises create value through research, development, and process refinement. Some, like Peter Drucker, have argued that the intellectual assets are the real basis of a company's value. If that is the case, then creating, controlling, and exploiting those intellectual assets are an essential business process. Portals play a key role in the knowledge management (KM) arena. In this chapter we examine key structures in successful KM initiatives:

- Search functions
- Metadata
- Expert directories

Searching across large and even moderate-sized repositories is much more challenging than many users first expect. By using some of the best practices outlined in this chapter you can avoid some common pitfalls. Taxonomies, or hierarchical organizations of categories, were popularized on the Web by Yahoo! (http://www.yahoo.com) and the Open Directory Project (http://www.dmoz.com). They complement keyword searching and provide another avenue for finding relevant content in a repository. Information about content in repositories, that is, metadata, is a support system that enables better information retrieval and content management. Finally, expert directories are emerging as an essential complement to more document-centric approaches to KM.

Before jumping into the details of these techniques, we briefly discuss three different types of information that KM systems encompass. The goal here is to clearly delineate where those techniques are applicable and where they are not. Later in this chapter we examine two case studies to explore how the best practices for exploiting these intellectual resources through the enterprise information portal were applied.

## Types of Information

KM portals provide access to three types of information:

1. Structured data
2. Unstructured data
3. Tacit knowledge

The differences between these makes the need for different management techniques clear.

### Structured Data

Most database applications deal with structured data. Transactional systems, like billing and claims processing, depend on specific pieces of information provided in well-defined formats. These systems support high volumes of activity and require that data not vary from a small range. When there is a potential for ambiguity, system designers assign artificial identifiers (e.g., customer IDs) to avoid any confusion. Online shoppers are accustomed to the familiar message "Enter the credit card holder's name exactly as it appears on the card." Transaction processing systems are not designed to determine whether "Joe Smith" and "Joseph Smith" are names of the same customer. Instead, the burden is on the user to provide unique identifiers or enter data unambiguously; in return, the transactional systems provide fast, scalable processing.

Similar restrictions apply to data warehousing and traditional analytic applications. Data moved from operational systems undergoes carefully planned transformations to ensure the centralized data warehouse or data mart has consistently formatted and encoded data, regardless of its original source. Applications like transaction processing systems and data warehouses are successful because their scope is limited and the data that enters the systems is highly controlled. We now realize that much of the information in organizations (some estimate as much as 80%) does not fit into the structured data models of transaction processing and data warehouses. This information is unstructured.

## Unstructured Data

Unstructured data management systems are pervasive. File systems, document management systems, e-mail, and intranets are all examples. Users find information in these systems by using a combination of techniques, including searching for keywords, and navigating organizational structures such as directory trees. In some cases, repositories support the use of parametric searches based on document type, dates, authors, and other metadata attributes. For example, an advanced search form might allow a user to search for all manuals that contain the phrase "High-temperature extrusion processes" and were published between June 1, 2002, and December 31, 2002.

By its nature, text, image, video, and audio data does not easily fit into relational models of entities. Of course, we can store documents, images, and video clips in databases and so in that sense they are structured. However, this misrepresents the value of these items because the true worth of a document lies in the collection of facts, opinions, and insights discussed in the text.

Consider a typical database entry for a status report stored in a document management system. The entry contains metadata about the document as shown below.

| | |
|---|---|
| Title: | Production Line Redesign Project—Status Report 01/10/03 |
| Author: | Mary Jones |
| Keywords: | redesign project; status report |
| Creation Date: | 01/10/03 |
| Summary: | Weekly project status report on redesign project; discusses issues with proposed extrusion process |

This metadata provides useful information but still does not reflect the key elements of the document, such as the exact issues with the proposed extrusion process. What about the processes? What are the risks of making the design change now? Are there known problems that need to be resolved? What will it cost? How long will it take to implement? These types of questions will vary by the topic of a document and we can never hope to create a fixed set of metadata attributes to answer all the possible questions for the entire database of documents. The only way to track these kinds of issues is to get inside the document and analyze the content.

Metadata is also used to more effectively manage image, video, and audio assets. Unfortunately, the tools available to analyze these data types are not as advanced as those we have for unstructured texts. Vendors are providing speech-to-text conversion programs and image matching and retrieval systems, but the effectiveness of these tools varies widely depending on the type of application. The single best practice when assessing search and analysis tools for images, video, and audio data sources is to test the tools in-house with your own data and determine whether the quality of service is sufficient to meet your business requirements.

Since the demand for image, video, and audio management is significantly less than that for unstructured text, and given the wide range of effectiveness of those tools, we will concentrate our discussion on unstructured texts.

### Tacit Knowledge

Structured and unstructured data management techniques are designed to connect people to data, but that does not always help. Sometimes you do not want to look up a structured record in a database or find a report or troubleshooting guide. Sometimes you just want to speak with someone who knows how to help solve a problem. The knowledge you need is walking around in someone's head. This tacit knowledge cannot be stored in a structured system, and even unstructured systems often cannot capture the full breadth of information someone knows about a particular issue. We can at best capture traces or footprints of this knowledge in collaboration systems, like threaded discussion systems, instant messaging logs, and e-mail exchanges. Using unstructured search techniques you might find a dialog in a discussion group between an expert and a coworker on a problem similar to your own. If you are fortunate, you might even have access to an expertise directory (see the NASA Jet Propulsion Lab case study later in this chapter for an example). No matter how it is done, whether by drawing inferences from dialogs or using expert directories, connecting people to people is the key to exploiting tacit knowledge.

Dealing with structured data is a well-developed IT area and certainly does not need any rehashing here. Instead we will focus on the role of unstructured and tacit knowledge in enterprise information portals. However, all three types of information—structured, unstructured, and tacit—are essential to the knowledge-intensive organization.

## Search Functions: The First Step

Search functions are common in unstructured data management systems. Web sites are routinely indexed using tools like Google (http://www.google.com) and ht://Dig (http://www.htdig.org) document management and e-mail systems provide search tools, and even relational databases are providing extensions to the relational engine to provide basic search services for unstructured content. This prevalence of search tools in different applications indicates one of the current problems with unstructured data: It is distributed across multiple platforms, often without a central point of access.

In most enterprises today, a knowledge worker has to know *where* to look for information as well as *what* to research. Considering that organizations routinely use shared file system drives, document management systems, e-mail public folders, intranet Web sites, and local hard drives to store key documents, the task of finding targeted information is daunting. Many users do not try or give up relatively quickly. According to a survey by Roper Starch Worldwide and commissioned by the search vendor WebTop, within just 12 minutes most users become frustrated when searching the Web [Sullivan 2001]. Frustration is probably comparable when searching internal resources. Enterprise information portals, however, can change this. Combined with an enterprise search facility, the portal can become the single point of access to content distributed across multiple platforms.

The first step to solving the enterprise search problem is to recognize that we will never create a single physical repository for all content. Our needs are too varied for a single tool. We can, however, develop a single logical view of enterprise content. Figure 8.1 depicts the basic architecture of enterprise search.

At the bottom of the figure we have the distributed repositories, which include file systems, e-mail public folders, document management systems, intranets, and external Web sources. Above the sources are gateways or middleware components that provide search engine access to the repositories. These gateways channel information between repositories and the search engine for spidering and query processes. The content index is a centralized database of information about content and usually includes full-text indexes of documents, metadata about those documents, and other proprietary information extracted and derived to improve the quality and effectiveness of searches. The top layer of the architecture diagram represents the user interface to the search engine.

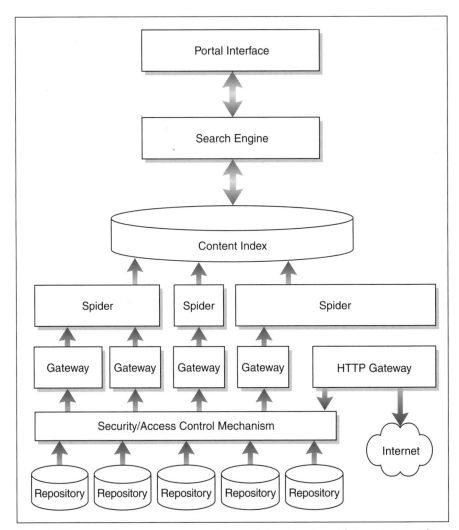

**Figure 8.1**     **Enterprise search requires an integrated architecture spanning content repositories, middleware connectivity, search engines, and user interfaces.**

We could fill an entire book delving into more detailed descriptions of each of these layers, but in the interest of sticking to the business basics, we will examine the two facets that require the most design decisions on the part of portal sponsors and architects: the search interface and the search engine configuration.

## What the Users See

The search interface can be relatively simple, such as a text box for entering a list of words to search. KM tools need advanced search services as well. These typically allow users to specify the following:

- The repositories to search, for example, just document management systems and shared files systems but not e-mail public folders
- Complex queries, such as "heat dissipation" <NEAR> "circuit" <AND> <NOT> "analog"
- Metadata parameters, such as the name of the author, the date of publication, or the owner department of the document
- Refinements to existing queries
- Stored queries to execute

Enterprise information portals should provide both simple and advanced search options. The former gives users quick access to a broad set of possibly useful documents while the advanced search allows users to refine queries and rapidly find information by specifying additional criteria. Sometimes eliminating information users do not want is as important as finding the information they do want.

## Search Engine Configuration

Search engine architectures range from the relatively simple to the complex. At one end of the spectrum we have search engines for static Web sites. These are easy to install and configure. The indexing process generally involves starting at a top-level home page and methodically following HTTP links to other pages in the site. At the other end of the spectrum we have enterprise search configurations with multiple repositories, different protocols, a range of file types, access control lists (ACLs), dynamically generated content, and a host of other contentious issues.

One of the key decisions that must be made when deploying enterprise search is how to distribute the search workload. Should a single type of search engine do all the work or should the work be divided among different types of search engines? In large enterprises, you will require multiple servers to index and respond to queries effectively, but you may have the opportunity to use search engines from several vendors. Choosing between a single-vendor or multiple-vendor environment will depend on several factors.

There are two basic architectural approaches to search systems: centralized and federated. In the centralized model, a single search application gathers content from multiple systems and maintains a centralized index. Figure 8.2 shows an example of a centralized search system.

In Figure 8.2 we show a single search engine, but conceivably there could be multiple instances of the same search engine software running on different servers. These servers are usually managed by a broker process that distributes the workload across the servers to maintain balanced performance.

Federated search systems, sometimes called brokered search systems, use multiple search engines to search distributed content. (The term *brokered* is used differently by vendors. In some cases it is used to describe a process that distributes tasks between instances of the same search engine, e.g., the Verity K2 Broker. In other cases a broker is a process that coordinates the work of different types of search engines, e.g., the Open Text Brokered Search Engine. To prevent confusion we will use the term *federated*.) One search engine accepts queries from users and

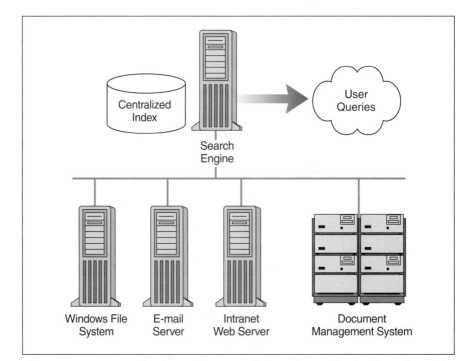

**Figure 8.2**    **A centralized search system is based on a single type of search engine.**

then passes them to the other search engines, which in turn provide result sets to the querying search engine. That search engine then combines the results and provides a combined list of results to the user. Figure 8.3 shows a typical federated environment.

Both models support two basic processes, indexing and querying. The indexing process begins when crawlers retrieve content from a target, such as a Web site, a network directory, or a document management folder. Figure 8.4 shows the typical stages of the crawling and indexing process. A crawler begins

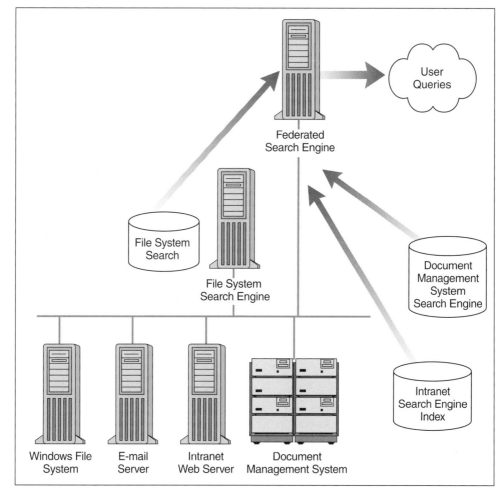

**Figure 8.3    A federated search system uses multiple search engines in a distributed environment.**

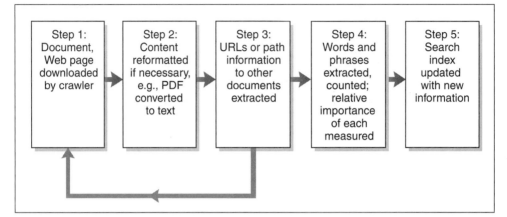

**Figure 8.4    Crawling and indexing are the first steps toward building and maintaining a search index.**

with a Web page or top-level directory and then follows links or subdirectories, gathering content in its path. As pages and documents are found, copies of their contents are sent back to the search server, which then preprocesses the data stream. Preprocessing is usually limited to extracting text from word processing, document publishing, spreadsheet, and presentation formatted files. Once the raw text has been extracted, it is indexed by any number of proprietary techniques. Simple indexing tools may catalog just frequency and location of words while others may extract complex patterns and information about the co-occurrence of terms to improve the quality of search results. Some search tools automatically extract and index metadata as well. The objective of these extra steps is to improve the quality of search.

### Improving the Quality of Search Results

Search quality is usually measured with two metrics: precision and recall. Precision is the measure of how well a search engine distinguishes documents that meet a user's query from those that do not. If a search engine returns only or almost only documents that meet a search query, precision is high; if it returns many irrelevant documents, precision is low. The second measure, recall, measures how well a search engine finds all documents that meet a query. If many relevant documents are missed, recall is low. Typically, search engines trade off precision for recall and vice versa. A search engine with high precision, that is, few irrelevant results, typically has lower recall, that is, it misses some documents that meet the query criteria. Similarly, if the search engine is tuned for high recall, the number of irrelevant documents tends to increase, leading to a lower precision.

How do we beat this problem? There are several approaches, but they all center around the need for providing additional information to the search engine.

One approach is to index metadata about documents. Metadata, especially keywords and descriptions, provides high-quality information to search engines. Terms in metadata are weighted more heavily than terms that appear just in the document body, under the assumption that the author of the document considers these metadata terms the most descriptive for the content. Metadata about the date the document was created or revised and information about the author can also be tracked by the search engine. This information then drives advanced search options such as searching for documents created between two dates, by a particular author, and containing certain keywords.

Another, more sophisticated approach involves tracking user behavior and modeling their interests. For example, the Verity K2 Recommendation engine analyzes user queries and search behaviors over time to find similarities between searchers. This information is then used to improve the quality of search by using information gained from users with similar interests. For example, if all users searching for "heat dissipation" articles read the same three articles, it is safe to assume that the next person searching for heat dissipation will also be interested in these, and the relative ranking of the documents should be increased to reflect that. This social network analysis is a relatively new approach to information retrieval and holds great promise. It is, however, a new technology, and it will need time to develop to full maturity.

## Frequently Encountered Enterprise Search Issues

Search is a complex process. Information is distributed across organizations, on multiple platforms, and in a variety of formats. To successfully deploy enterprise search, portal designers need to map out gateways to key repositories, address security and access control issues, and assess the tradeoffs between centralized and federated search systems.

### Gateways

Gateways are the glue that holds the enterprise search mechanism in place. Gateways allow crawlers to access content repositories as easily as they access http—at least, that is the goal. Gateways are typically required for document management systems, e-mail servers, and, in some cases, Web sites that rely heavily on dynamically generated content. During the retrieval process, gateways are responsible for finding documents or target content selected by a user and streaming it to the user's interface. Postprocessing steps, like highlighting search terms, may also depend on gateway functionality. Gateways are customized to particular applications or repositories and frequently depend on published APIs to the repositories. Keep in mind that upgrading a document management system or e-mail server that is indexed by the enterprise search engine might entail an upgrade of the gateway as well.

*Security*

Security is a factor in any enterprise application, and a search system is no different. Single sign-on services minimize the time-consuming and tedious task of logging into multiple repositories to retrieve documents and should be used in enterprise search systems when possible. Some search tools can cache user credentials and present them to multiple repositories, providing something of a middle ground between single sign-on and multiple user logins. The assumption is that a user has the same username and password on multiple repositories. Once users are authenticated against individual repositories, they can retrieve content listed in search results.

Perhaps the most challenging security issues in enterprise search revolve around how content is added to the index and how it is displayed to users who may not have access rights to view that content. Consider the following scenario. A crawler searches a document management system with access to all folders in a department's area. The crawler and indexer create entries for each document in the central index. A user enters a query and the search engine produces a list of matching documents. Should the search engine display a list of all those documents without checking access controls or should it verify that the user has read access to each before including it in the hit list?

Choosing either one of these options entails tradeoffs. If all documents are displayed, a searcher may learn of the existence of a document he or she cannot read and should not know about (e.g., All Salaries.xls). The benefit of this approach is simplicity. There are no extra steps to validate access rights. Checking access rights requires synchronizing ACLs between the repository and the search engine. This requires an additional process that must be monitored and maintained, and there is also the chance that the ACLs may get out of synchronization. The final decision depends on the particular benefits and risks to your organization.

*Centralized versus Federated Search Systems*

Earlier in the chapter we briefly discussed the difference between centralized and federated search systems. Now it is time to address the tradeoffs between the two.

A centralized search system provides a single index for all searchable content. It also provides the means to track, in fine-grained detail, the operations that users perform, the documents they read, and other related characteristics of their search behavior. This information in turn can be analyzed, along with other users' behaviors, to develop models of users' interests across the enterprise. A federated search system, however, does not centrally track this information. Instead, it divides the work of indexing and retrieving across multiple tools that have the ability to share queries and results. The key advantage of a federated search system is that each repository's search engine will most effectively implement search functions for its own platform. A document management system's search engine is designed with its security model in mind and best understands how to exploit metadata about documents to optimize the search and retrieval process. As with security, the better approach for your organization depends on a balance of the benefits and drawbacks of each.

Some multiple repositories have tightly related content; for example, an engineering department may use a document management system, several shared network drives, an intranet site, and some public e-mail folders as its repositories. In this case, a centralized approach is appropriate because the volume of content at the department level will not tax an enterprise search engine; the number of users is manageable; and the users and content probably share many similarities, lending themselves to social network analysis and other higher-level functions available in a centralized index. A large multinational company that has grown by merger and acquisition may have widely disparate document stores that cover a broad range of topics and entail millions of documents. In this case, a federated approach offers the better performance without sacrificing functionality because the range of content and users does not lend itself to higher-level analysis.

## Metadata: Know What It's All About

Metadata is a popular yet complex topic in the IT realm. *Metadata Solutions* by Adrienne Tannenbaum [2002] provides an in-depth discussion of the topic, especially in relation to structured data applications. For our purposes, however, we will examine a narrow range of the metadata topics and focus primarily on describing the content and services available within an enterprise portal. The driving reason to adopt a metadata strategy is to improve users' access to information and services they need to get their jobs done—and that means we need metadata about both content and applications.

Portal designers often consider content metadata but neglect to include information about the applications available to portal users. One of the best practices we have found is the use of metadata to describe services available to users from applications already deployed on portals. These applications range from simple administrative tools, such as those for expense report filing, to analytic services from data warehouse reporting tools. Successful enterprise portals make extensive use of metadata. The first step to incorporate metadata is to define standards for content and applications.

## Content Metadata

Most portals use content metadata to varying degrees. Figure 8.5 shows a typical simple metadata form for adding content to a portal. This is similar to the basic metadata attributes tracked in desktop applications like Microsoft Word.

Although metadata entry forms provide the means to track similar data, they do not use a standardized set of terms. This is a common problem that should not be allowed in a portal. The first step to managing metadata is to define a standard set of metadata attributes.

The Dublin Core (http://www.dublincore.org) is a widely recognized metadata standard for Web resources that contains the following main elements:

- Title: the title of the document
- Creator: the primary developer of the content
- Subject and Keywords: the main topics or themes
- Description: a brief description of the content
- Publisher: the person or organization making the content available
- Contributor: the person or organization adding content to the document or resource
- Date: the date associated with significant events, such as creation and retirement of the resource
- Resource Type: an indication of the kind of resource, for example, text, sound, image, or software
- Format: the media type of the content

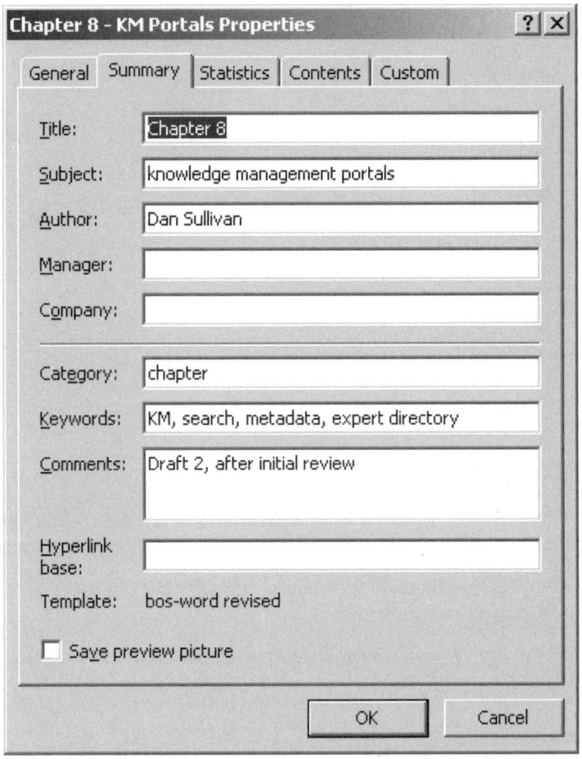

Figure 8.5    Metadata management begins at the point of document creation and can be initiated with basic properties managed by desktop applications.

- Resource Identifier: the Universal Resource Identifier (URI) of the resource
- Source: an identifier indicating the formal source of the content
- Language: an indication of the language of the document, typically a two-letter abbreviation using the ISO 639 and ISO 3166 standards
- Relation: a reference to a related resource
- Coverage: usually a name of a location, time, or jurisdiction
- Rights Management: a description of the intellectual property rights of the resource

The Dublin Core is a good starting point for a portal metadata standard if you select the core elements that are most useful for your site. All 15 elements and their variations are not required in most cases, and I recommend limiting the number of required elements to 6 or fewer whenever possible. The following make a good beginning:

- Title
- Creator
- Subject
- Description
- Creation Date
- Expiration Date

After selecting a set of attributes, a portal designer must decide how to implement the standard. In most cases, the format of a document or the content repository dictates the choice. For example, Microsoft uses a proprietary properties format, and HTML pages can use HTTP META tags or XML-based metadata schemes, such as the Resource Description Format (RDF). Document management systems may have proprietary methods as well. Fortunately, search engine gateways should provide a method to extract metadata from a content repository and add it to a centralized content index, where it is exploited by the search engine. Extracting metadata occurs at the same times as full-text indexing and provides the opportunity to map different naming conventions into a standardized form. Those standard attribute names should be used consistently as labels in advanced search forms. In the case of federated searches, application-specific search engines should have ready access to the metadata used in those repositories.

Too often, users do not bother to enter information into these fields, and the opportunity to improve the quality of search and retrieval is lost. To minimize this impact, make the process of adding metadata as simple as possible. Use drop-down lists whenever possible. Develop a list of valid terms for subject keywords (known as a controlled vocabulary). Automatically provide default values for creation and expiration dates. A search engine's summary-generating program can provide a default description that users can edit and refine prior to saving a document. Not all metadata can be automatically generated (if it could, we wouldn't need it), but we can provide some aid to users who feel they need fewer, not more, demands on their time.

## Application Metadata

When looking for information, it may not be in a document or Web page but in an application or structured database. At these times it is essential to have access to a repository of metadata about applications. Within this repository, we should track the following attributes for each application available through the portal:

- Application Name
- Application Owner
- Administrator/Point of Contact
- Vendor Name
- Purpose
- Databases Used
- Used By
- Platform
- Related Applications
- Application URL
- Link to Documentation

The application metadata repository should be indexed by the enterprise search engine. A number of platforms are suitable for application metadata: a directory of XML files, a relational database, and a document management system with XML files all suffice. For a small number of applications, a directory of XML files, one for each application, is the easiest to implement. If a large number of applications must be tracked, issues such as version control and concurrency control become more important, and a database or document management system approach is called for.

---

**CASE STUDY: Johnson Controls Manages Information Overload with Metadata**

Johnson Controls, Inc., headquartered in Milwaukee, Wisconsin, with offices in 40 countries, is a global market leader in automotive systems and facility management and control; sales in 2002 totaled $20.1 billion. The $5 billion Controls Group of Johnson Controls, Inc., offers customers unmatched expertise and facility solutions to make nonresidential facilities perform better, resulting in improved comfort, safety, energy efficiency, and employee productivity. With the need to provide information to 12,000 sales, engineering, manufacturing, and support personnel, Johnson Controls became an early adopter of Internet technologies for content management. In 1996 the company initiated the Advisor project to provide a single point of access to essential company documents for its employees.

**The Problem: Managing Growing Content**

Under the direction of Jim Smith, the Advisor intranet manager and Web master for the Controls Group, the company implemented a custom-developed portal application using Perl and Common Gateway Interface (CGI) techniques and later using Java. Johnson Controls quickly realized the need to search across multiple document types and selected Verity Information Server to provide search services. While this met the company's needs at first, as the amount of content grew, Johnson Controls realized that maintenance issues could undermine the success of the project. Content was duplicated, users lost track of documents of record, and obsolete information continued to accumulate in the repository. As the amount of indexed content grew, so did the result sets returned to users—and too often those results included irrelevant information.

Users were facing two common problems with Web-based searching. First, documents relevant to a user's search were not identified because of a difference in terms. For example, someone searching for the acronym "HVAC" (heating, ventilation, and air conditioning) would be interested in documents containing the phrase "heating, ventilation, and air conditioning" as well as those containing "HVAC." Keyword-based searches would miss this. The second problem was that too much information was returned to users. Sales staff and engineers both search for information about particular products but with different intentions. Salespersons are more likely to be interested in product literature and brochures while engineers would prefer technical specifications and production details. Neither group is interested in the other documents.

Smith and the Advisor developers realized they needed to focus as much on eliminating content that users do not need as on finding content they do need. The solution to these problems centered on adding metadata about the topic and form of documents.

**The Solution: Metadata**

Metadata, or information about the content stored in the repository, provided both users and administrators with additional details they needed to work more effectively.

The Advisor team members analyzed Web logs and found that document types, such as brochure, template, product sheet, and recall notices, were frequently requested. They also understood that users worked in four broad areas (sales, engineering, service, and general employee services) and that they discussed issues related to three topics (customers, products, and employees). The team now had three dimensions to help restrict search: document type, work area, and general topic. When users search, in addition to using keywords, they can specify details for each criterion, such as search only for product sheets in the sales domain. For example, a salesperson could now search for brochures on temperature controls and receive sales and marketing information without being inundated with engineering diagrams and specifications.

By searching and browsing in general topic areas, such as HVAC, users are more likely to find what they need. Multiple terms for the same idea can still be problematic, but with a controlled vocabulary for defining topics, users are much more likely to find what they want, even if they do not know every possible way of describing their interests.

Administrators as well as users benefited from the use of metadata. With a mechanism for storing arbitrary details about content, system managers could define access control information, document retention rules, and other administrative details. One of the most useful details is the expiration date. When new content is added to the repository, it is automatically assigned an expiration date. When the date approaches, the system notifies the owner of the content that the document is about to expire unless he or she takes some action. If the owner does not renew the document, it is archived on the expiration date and no longer available in search results. If 60 days past the expiration date the owner still does not want the content in the repository, that document is deleted.

The Advisor team started with basic metadata but then adopted a widely used Web standard, the Dublin Core. (See the Content Metadata subsection in this chapter for more information on the Dublin Core.)

### Return on Investment

Like so many portal and KM applications, calculating ROI is a challenge. The focus on metrics led Smith and other members of the Advisor development group to implement a metadata strategy as a solution to the problems users and administrators were facing. Following the same interest in quantitative analysis, the team measured the two metrics that could easily be tracked: size of result sets and time spent searching. With the addition of metadata, the average result set was reduced 90%. Considering that most users never look past the first 20 to 30 hits, such a drop in the number of possible hits greatly increases the chance that users will find what they are looking for. Through user surveys, the team found that users saved on average one hour per day with the new search tools. Smith is quick to point out, however, that this does not translate into bottom-line savings on employee costs; it simply means that users have more time for other tasks. In some cases, productivity increases; in other cases, users do not extend their work days into overtime hours.

**Lessons Learned**

The Advisor application needs to serve a wide and diverse audience at Johnson Controls. By analyzing users' interactions with search tools, the development team was able to find logical patterns that reflected the way users think about searching and then used metadata to support those models. Explicit information about content improves both the quality of searches and the overall administration of the system. By adopting a widely used standard, Johnson Controls avoided reinventing the metadata wheel and benefited from the extensive work done by the Dublin Core group. Metadata has improved the quality of searches as measured by both objective Web log analysis and through subjective surveys of users' perceived time savings.

Content used with permission of Johnson Controls.

## Expert Directories: Connecting People to People

So far we have described how to search portals for information contained in unstructured texts and for services available through applications. As for tacit knowledge, that hard-to-define but essential intellectual asset that roams the halls and offices of organizations inside the heads of knowledge workers, we need to turn to expert directories.

Expert directories are semistructured databases of information about knowledge workers' experience, projects, training, and formal education. Resumes provide a starting point for expert directories, but more detailed, concrete information is needed than is generally available in these documents. In particular, an expert directory should include the following:

- Detailed descriptions of projects undertaken
- Unusual challenges faced in projects

- Recognized areas of expertise
- Management responsibilities
- Availability to answer questions and consult with others

Remember, someone can be an expert without having a Ph.D. and several patents under his or her name. An expert has specific knowledge about an organization's processes, operations, products, and services and, most importantly, is willing to share that knowledge with others. Always confer with employees and consultants before including them in the expert directory to ensure they are willing and able to provide assistance to others. Overworked experts, no matter how knowledgeable, are of no use if they don't return cold calls from coworkers.

## CASE STUDY: NASA JPL's Federated Knowledge Management Architecture

The National Aeronautics and Space Administration's Jet Propulsion Laboratory (NASA JPL), based in Pasadena, California, is the space agency's primary center for robotic space exploration. The Lab, operated by the California Institute of Technology, is the home to a diverse staff, including physicists, engineers, managers, and anthropologists. These professionals collaborate on NASA JPL's efforts, which range from exploring known planets in the solar system (they've sent spacecraft to all except Pluto) and collecting particles from solar winds to testing ion engines and autonomous guidance systems in deep space explorers. There is even a mission called Deep Impact planned to launch in 2004 that will hurl a projectile at Temple 1 to study the composition and structure of the comet. Although these exotic projects have challenges most of us do not need to address, for example, projects that last decades, they also have much in common with our more usual, worldly projects.

### The Problem: Managing Knowledge Across the Organization

Like many corporations, NASA needed to address the problems that arise with searches, metadata management, and expert directories. NASA JPL's projects, called missions, are

- **Knowledge intensive**
- **High risk**
- **Capital intensive**
- **Relatively few in number**

We find these same characteristics in projects for industries such as defense, oil exploration, and pharmaceutical research. NASA decided to harness KM techniques to better manage and communicate knowledge across the organization, thus improving mission performance and cutting development costs. NASA JPL's KM project adopted a federated architecture for providing the infrastructure and services needed to meet its objectives. The architecture is a model for large, knowledge-intensive organizations in any domain.

### The Solution: Federated Knowledge Management Architecture

NASA JPL identified three essential elements of a successful KM architecture:

1. Services
2. Processes
3. Systems

Services address core operations that integrate users and resources, such as document management, identity management, and metadata management. Processes are the operations that address JPL's day-to-day operations and are supported by better system integration and the use of expert systems. The systems element includes portals, collaboration tools, and knowledge capture mechanisms.

The portal system provides the single point of access to the services and processes JPL researchers and engineers need. The portal's feature set includes the aggregation of resources that hold meaning for the user as well as the ability to customize the portal desktop page. Users can create a personal start page that reflects their work, professional interests, and organizational needs. In addition, the portal brings in headlines automatically from external Web space, which allows employees to easily track new developments in their field.

Simply providing access to multiple applications from a single point, however, is not enough. A deep, user-centric integration is required. JPL is using effective search systems, browse taxonomies, and metadata to ensure the intellectual assets of the organization are highly accessible. (There are many other relevant aspects of NASA's federated KM architecture that are beyond the scope of this case study. See Jeanne Holm's detailed overview at https://partners-lib.jpl.nasa.gov/partners-lib/dscgi/ds.py/View/Collection-17.)

*Search Systems*

The KM team members knew that a single point of access through a portal and extensive search functionality were starting points for their efforts. With an eventual rollout to 5,500 JPL employees that would include internal resources as well as over 4,000,000 publicly available Web pages, scalability was a key design consideration. After an extensive period of gathering user requirements and product research, the NASA JPL KM Navigation Team chose the Sun iPlanet Portal (since renamed Sun One Portal Server).

The Laboratory evaluated a number of commercial and open source search products before eventually selecting Google. Although speed and scalability were obvious considerations in the selection, the quality of search results was also a key factor. Google's emphasis on hyperlink properties and its use of page citations as a result-ranking mechanism lend themselves to NASA JPL's intranet environment and provide the kind of intuitive results users expect. For example, when a user searches for "Mars," the Mars group home page appears at the top of the result set. Even after finding an appropriate search tool (there is no single best search system), the KM team found there was still plenty of work to do: configuring crawlers, eliminating loops in hyperlink paths, and performing other tasks that are necessary to exploit the full potential of enterprise search.

The search problem is compounded by the many different types of formats and data types found in JPL Web space. In this regard, JPL is no different than any other large company or organization. The use of metasearch is now being explored as a way to leverage the efforts of different kinds of search that are particularly well suited to different types of data. The goal is to provide a single point of query access that spans many different databases and other collections of files and documents.

*Browse Taxonomies*

Search systems are just one way to make information accessible through a portal. Navigating through a browsable Web directory is another proven technique. Yahoo! and the Open Directory Project popularized Web directories and taxonomies. For large-scale enterprise information portals, such as NASA JPL's, they are essential.

The team began its task of creating an institutional Web Space Directory by doing extensive customer research involving card-sorting exercises and use case scenarios. In one instance, users were asked to organize note cards labeled with categories into hierarchies; in another, users were observed while they tried to find particular pieces of information using a test taxonomy. The team finally settled on a taxonomy after it completed seven rounds of usability testing. The resulting taxonomy is included on the Inside JPL portal as the JPL Web Space Directory.

The team also included its research from studying the logs generated by users' search queries. The logs clarified which Web sites users needed most and what languages they used. This gave the team important clues about "trigger words" and how JPL employees think about their virtual workspace. The creation of an underlying information architecture that gives meaning and context to JPL Web space is the ultimate goal of the taxonomy group.

The tests do not mark the end of the taxonomy development process. Once the Inside JPL portal rolls out to its entire internal customer base, user feedback and comments will provide critical information about how the institutional taxonomy should grow. In addition, a technical taxonomy is yet to be created. There is no final step in this development; taxonomies are organic structures that will continue to grow and change as the organizational knowledge changes. The NASA JPL team is clearly focused on developing methods to manage that growth and adapt to those changes. The team also recognized that different parts of the taxonomy require different development strategies.

A separate strategy that the team is following is to create specific data channels incorporated into the portal that are tailored to different user groups by work family. Hence, there are channels that contain "mini browse directories" of electronic resources for each of the following groups: scientists, engineers, and business staff. These role-based link collections were gathered by representatives from the groups themselves. The team is watching the popularity and use of these channels in order to plan the next steps in their development.

It is worth noting that NASA JPL did not try to discover a taxonomy by using one of the many automatic categorization and taxonomy development tools on the market. Once the taxonomy is sufficiently refined, the KM team will use automatic categorizers to classify existing content.

### Metadata

Categories and taxonomies are just one type of metadata commonly used in enterprise portals. NASA JPL uses the Dublin Core metadata standard with site-specific additions, creating a set of 15 attributes. The Lab requires only 5 attributes for content; the other 10 are optional. Currently, metadata is kept along with HTML in Web pages, however, implementation is voluntary and inconsistent. Eventually the Lab plans to separate content and metadata with the use of a Web content management system. The content will remain distributed across the organization and over multiple platforms. Metadata about specific documents, Web pages, and images are developing into XML schemas that are more flexible than current metadata attributes and represent the first steps toward automated Web publishing.

NASA JPL generates, manages, searches, and navigates terabytes of information, from planetary images to geological formations. This data can make or break a mission so the lab has a pressing need to make it accessible across the organization. NASA JPL is now wrestling with metadata about repositories. For example, if a user queries for "Images from Mars," the query should not be sent blindly to all federated search engines but targeted to image databases and reformulated to a query suitable for those databases. This type of intelligent middleware in the search infrastructure pushes the limits of existing search tools and marks one of the next-generation features forthcoming in enterprise search.

### When Search and Navigation Systems Are Not Enough

Search systems are useful for finding answers to targeted questions, and global navigation structures help when users have general areas of interest, but sometimes questions are too broad and needs too large for these techniques. NASA JPL developed two alternative methods for knowledge sharing along these broader dimensions. The first is an expertise finding directory and the other is a technical questions database.

The expertise finding directory, called Know Who, contains profiles of 1,100 technical experts who can answer questions or work on projects. As with the taxonomy development, a manual approach was used to populate the expert database. Experts in different domains were identified and consulted about inclusion in the directory. The KM team members realized that they needed to respect organizational culture and personal preferences when developing this service. Professionals, no matter how knowledgeable, will not offer much help if they are too busy for or unaccustomed to calls from strangers with pressing technical problems. They can, however, share their expertise indirectly through the technical questions database.

NASA JPL conducts regular technical reviews of missions with an eye to spotting potential problems. The technical questions database consists of over 700 questions in 42 subject areas that are often raised during mission reviews. Designers and project managers access these questions and answers to discover issues or problems that could hamper their missions.

NASA JPL has created a KM environment based on key functions like search, navigation, and expertise finding that complements and fits within the organization's widespread, federated information infrastructure.

## Best Practices

Like most projects at NASA JPL, the KM initiative is a long-term prospect. Success is predicated on crafting services to the way people work and meeting the needs of individuals, teams, and projects. Within the realm of KM-oriented enterprise information portals we find several best practices at NASA JPL.

- **Expect a prolonged deployment for enterprise search.** Search is difficult—no two ways about it. Expect to evaluate a number of different search tools before finding one that works well in your environment. Also, plan to configure and administer the search engine, and be ready for unexpected problems and cleanup work with the intranet.
- **Begin taxonomies with existing structures familiar to users.** Academic classification schemes are sound organizations of knowledge, but they do not always work well in commercial and government organizations where professionals from a wide range of backgrounds need to collaborate and share information. The most important consideration in the building of taxonomies is to identify the ways your customers think about the data they use. The JPL KM Navigation Team used mental modeling and goal mapping to find out more about how their users think and how they prefer to retrieve electronic information. File systems, document management systems, existing Web sites, and other information management systems within an organization reflect intuitive or at least de facto hierarchical schemes that users have developed. Use these as starting points for devising taxonomies, but do not assume they are ideal or will work as well in an enterprise portal as they do in other systems. Work with users to test the efficacy of the taxonomy for navigation in an iterative process that refines classification of information.

- **Design metadata about repositories as well as content.** Metadata within documents is used to improve the quality of results in some search engines and provides the basis for parametric searches. Define a metadata standard and look to public standards such as the Dublin Core as a starting point. Deploy metadata in a manner that advances the long-term goal of making information accessible. In a Web-only environment, this could mean keeping metadata in HTML pages. In environments with a strong document and content management presence, metadata can be distributed among the different repositories, assuming your search engine can index those metadata stores. Finally, in widely varying enterprises with multiple types of data stores, a centralized metadata repository should be considered.
- **Make tacit knowledge accessible through an expert directory.** Keep in mind that explicit knowledge comprises only a fraction of the total intellectual assets of an organization. Also, portal users looking for solutions to problems are not necessarily interested in a dissertation on the topic; they just want answers. Some experts with the skills and knowledge worth including in such a service will not want to participate. Include information about both general academic and professional experience as well as specific project details in an expertise directory.

## Conclusion

Managing knowledge is an elusive goal. Enterprise portals are one way of capturing and sharing best practices, lessons learned, and contact information for experts. Both NASA JPL and Johnson Controls demonstrated that, as elusive as KM may be, attempting to realize the goal produces tangible benefits. When designing a KM portal, assume that developing a high-quality, enterprise-level search service will require significant effort. Pay close attention to developing sustainable metadata standards that will be adopted by those who add content to the portal. When metadata is available to a search engine, the quality of search can improve significantly. Also, remember that tacit knowledge will never be captured electronically. Sometimes the best answer to a problem is found in a dialogue with another employee, not in a document repository. A methodical approach and patience are essential to building the most challenging of all types of portals, the KM system.

# References

Sullivan, Danny. 2001. "WebTop Search Rage Study." Accessed in June 2003 at
*http://searchenginewatch.com/sereport/article.php/2163351.*

Tannenbaum, Adrienne. 2002. *Metadata Solutions: Using Metamodels, Repositories, XML and Enterprise Portals to Generate Information on Demand.* Boston, MA: Addison-Wesley.

# PART III

# Building Your Own Proven Portal

# CHAPTER NINE

# Five Common Themes in Proven Portals

Throughout this book we have examined design principles in both theory and practice. In this chapter, we describe in detail five themes common to successful portal implementations:

1. Focus on business processes
2. Emphasis on ease of use
3. Deep integration of applications
4. Scalability of services
5. Well-developed security models

These five themes appear to varying degrees in proven portals. Customer-facing portals stress all these themes while KM portals require more emphasis on ease of use and integration than on a particular business process. These five themes will play a role in your own well-designed portal.

## Focus on Business Processes

Portals hold many advantages over delivering stand-alone applications in mainframe or client/server environments, but unless the portal deployment is in service to specific business processes, those benefits will not be realized. Organizations should introduce portals to solve specific problems—they should not introduce a portal and then look for a problem. As counterintuitive as it sounds, this practice is all too common. It has even gotten to the point that portal vendors are asking customers and prospects, "Is your portal as empty as a dorm-room fridge?" [Plumtree Software 2003]. The first step in deploying a proven portal is defining the business problem to address.

What constitutes an appropriate problem for a portal solution? First, the problem must be related to a core business operation, like serving customers or managing production. Deploying a portal so users can check their e-mail from the Web, read the latest company press release, look up flight information, or monitor stock prices is not enough. Most successful portals include these services, but the portals are not driven by them. A second characteristic of appropriate problems is that they require multiple applications. Empire Blue Cross Blue Shield (see Chapter 3) and the Institute for Healthcare Improvement (see Chapter 6) needed to provide agents and customers with consolidated access to information from a number of different systems. They chose different implementation models based on their businesses requirements, but both used portals as the organizing framework. Third, business operations that have workflow elements are well served by portals. Finally, any process that supports searching for information distributed across multiple repositories or delivering personalized reports should be deployed in a portal. KM and business intelligence systems are best deployed through portals.

Portals have demonstrably improved a number of processes, with measurable effects:

- Reducing time to deliver services
- Reducing time to resolve disputes
- Consolidating service delivery across channels
- Providing analytic services and specialized tools to support operations
- Providing a single point of access to multiple content repositories

As the case studies in this book demonstrate, when the business drives the technology, the organization realizes real returns on investment and avoids the career-killing "empty portal" syndrome.

## Emphasis on Ease of Use

The need to make portal use intuitive and convenient cannot be overstated. Of course, users will have different ideas about what constitutes "intuitive" and "convenient," but we can get consensus on 80% of ease-of-use factors by adopting a few design principles.

- Keep a user-centric perspective.
- Personalize the services offered.
- Follow recognized design patterns.
- Use a single sign-on service.

A customer-centric perspective means designing the portal around how users think about the business processes supported by the portal. Conversely, it means not designing the portal based on the implementation of underlying systems. For example, a customer making an online purchase thinks in terms of finding products, adding them to a shopping cart, and checking out. The underlying implementation requires the coordination of inventory, content management, credit processing, and a host of other steps that are irrelevant to a user's perspective. When the implementation details of enterprise architecture are exposed to a user (e.g., a claim status is not available because the batch process handling won't complete for a few hours), we have violated the user-centric perspective.

Services should be personalized to each user. For example, when shopping for auto parts, users want the portal to remember details about their cars. At myHalliburton (see Chapter 6), engineers and geologists can explicitly define their areas of interest, which in turn drive the suite of technical applications and utilities available to them through the portal. Personalization is an effective way to keep a user-centric perspective.

The Web is mature enough now that designers have discovered design patterns that work across different applications of portals. Some of these, described in Chapter 1, include active links, which provide a sense of location within large sites, and navigation neighborhoods, which create easily navigated subareas of a site. In addition to navigation patterns, information modelers have discovered the power of faceted models of content. These models describe metadata attributes about content, such as document type, areas of interest, time of publication, and other dimensions along which we can categorize documents. These are powerful models because they support information retrieval the way users think about it. "I'm looking for the policy document from HR published sometime in the last two years that talked about leave time." Faceted models are used to augment conventional keyword searching, which is also ubiquitous in well-designed portals. Searching for keywords even within an internal portal can yield thousands of results, but when a search engine also has information about facets, the quality of searches increase dramatically and the number of hits drops significantly. (See the Johnson Controls case study in Chapter 8 for more on metadata and search systems.)

Single sign-on services are one of the most important techniques for improving security while making portal use more convenient. These services allow users to log into the portal once and then have access to other applications with separate authentication mechanisms. This minimizes the number of passwords a user has to remember and lessens the likelihood of users writing down their passwords or using the same passwords repeatedly.

Ease of use is a key factor in portal adoption, and the full potential of the portal might not be realized without it.

## Deep Integration of Applications

Portals offer the opportunity to integrate applications in a number of ways. In Chapter 2 we discussed the basic three-tier architecture of portals: the presentation layer, the application server layer, and the data services layer. The presentation layer, by default, integrates multiple applications with links to a variety of programs and services. The applications themselves do not share data and are integrated only in the sense that they are available from a single point. This is shallow integration. Deep integration, on the other hand, occurs at the application server or data services layers.

Deep integration at the application server layer tends to focus on data exchange services, often in an XML format. Web services are growing in popularity for application server integration because of their flexibility in adopting to a wide range of needs and the broad acceptance of implementation standards such as SOAP, WSDL, and, to a less extent, UDDI. Web services support loosely coupled integration and allow underlying applications to change without necessarily changing the interface between systems.

Deep integration at the data services layer involves more tightly integrated exchanges of data, often using enterprise application integration services, such as IBM MQ Series messaging servers, to exchange data between databases and to keep them in logically consistent states. Some techniques (e.g., database replication) are closely tied to the database implementation, and changes in one system require changes in the others or in the replication process.

From our point of view as portal designers, both types of deep integration support the delivery of business processes. For example, an e-commerce portal could use a Web service to check inventory levels on a product, verify a customer's credit, and calculate local sales tax, all behind the scenes from the user's perspective. Deep integration is one of the techniques required to develop portals from a user-centric perspective.

## Scalability of Services

All portal designers want to see their systems widely adopted and used to deliver essential services to their organizations. Be careful what you wish for. Portals, like other heavily used applications, need to scale to meet user needs. Potential bottle-necks are found throughout a portal environment:

- Web servers
- Application servers
- Database servers
- Network infrastructure

Web servers can become overloaded with traffic without load-balancing devices to spread the load across a number of servers. Fortunately, this type of load balancing is well understood, and there are a number of different architectural approaches to the problem [Bourke 2001].

The demands on application servers are more complex than those on Web servers, but again load balancing across multiple servers can maintain service levels. Clustering servers creates a single logical compute resource from a set of separate servers and allows for the addition of more servers as demand dictates. Clustering can be done at the operating system level, as with Linux, or at the application server level, as with Zope Enterprise Objects (the distributed object system for the Zope application server).

Database servers have long wrestled with scalability concerns. Market leaders like Oracle and IBM support an array of features to improve performance. Open source databases, especially MySQL, have made performance a top priority and are now beginning to provide both speed and essential features such as referential integrity and stored procedures. Maintaining a scalable database for portals requires the same level of design and implementation tuning required by other data-intensive applications.

Network infrastructure encompasses services from Internet access and firewalls to single sign-on and authorization services. Spikes in the demand for network resources can occur for a number of reasons. Traffic to an e-commerce site can spike during promotional periods and peak sales seasons. KM portals can put high demands on file servers and network bandwidth when indexing content for the portal search engine.

The developers of proven portals, having recognized these potential bottlenecks, deploy the necessary hardware and design and tune the software as needed to sustain expected growth in the portal.

## Well-Developed Security Models

Since portals provide access to a multitude of applications, often over the Internet and at least over an intranet, it is important to maintain tight system security. Many successful portals use a combination of techniques:

- Identity management and single sign-on services
- Enterprise directories
- Role-based access schemes
- Rule-based access schemes

Identity management and single sign-on services are some of the most promising benefits of portals. These services ease administration, reduce help desk support calls, and make it easier to use applications. Enterprise directories support identity and authorization systems by providing a centralized source of information on individual and group attributes. These attributes are in turn used to manage roles assigned to individual users (e.g., Joe Smith is a member of the Manager group) and rules defined to control the use of resources (e.g., Directory \\server1\finance\audit is available only during business hours and to members of the Audit Committee group). As portals provide a framework to integrate applications, they must also integrate security mechanisms that protect those applications and their resources.

## Conclusion

Successful portals share common features. They solve real business problems, keep their focus on the user, use deep integration, design for growth while maintaining performance, and keep the portal and constituent applications secure through centralized enterprise identity management and security controls. Depending on the type of portal, these features vary in importance.

In the next chapter we will shift our focus away from identifying key characteristics of well-designed portals to outlining the steps required to design and build your own proven portal.

## References

Bourke, Tony. 2001. *Server Load Balancing.* Cambridge, MA: O'Reilly.
Plumtree Software. 2003. "No Empty Portals! Workshop Series." Accessed in June 2003 at *http://www.plumtree.com/reg/fs/noemptyportals/.*

# CHAPTER TEN

# Implementing Your Proven Portal

Throughout this book we have discussed principles of portal design, documented best practices, and seen them used in case studies of proven portals. Now it is time to turn our attention to designing and deploying your own portal. In this chapter we outline a road map to take you from recognizing the need for a portal to implementing and maintaining a sustainable, well-adopted system. There are four basic steps in this process.

1. Understand the business drivers.
2. Design the portal.
3. Assess the ROI.
4. Incrementally implement and adapt the portal.

Following these four steps may not guarantee success—there are many risk factors outside a designer's control—but this process will ensure that you avoid some all-too-common mistakes.

## Understanding the Business Drivers

The first step in deploying a portal is to understand the problem it will solve. Most organizations have multiple reasons for using a portal. In some cases, enterprises are looking for operational efficiencies. Halliburton reduced the time required to resolve billing disputes (see Chapter 6). Empire Blue Cross Blue Shield reduced the time required to generate policies and improved the rate of claims approvals (see Chapter 3). These process-oriented portals delivered real value because the portal's functionality was designed for a specific process. However, in some cases, the process is not the problem.

Collaboration is another top business driver behind the rise of portals. The intellectual assets of an organization are as important as or more important than the tangible assets of many businesses. CARE Canada has no factories or manufacturing equipment; its most valuable assets are the knowledge and experience of their disaster relief teams (see Chapter 4). NASA's Jet Propulsion Laboratory has plenty of hardware and scientific equipment, but take away the scientists and engineers and it's no longer the JPL (see Chapter 8). Even Johnson Controls, a leading manufacturer, is dependent on the collaboration features of its portal to share sales, engineering, and operational information across the organization (see Chapter 8). The functional requirements of collaboration systems are generally looser than those of process-oriented portals.

Of course, portals are used for both streamlining business processes and collaboration, but the requirements gathering process is different so we will examine the steps separately.

## Gathering Requirements for Process-Oriented Portals

The first step to deploying process support in a portal is understanding the existing process and the users' general requirements. The following questions can help identify salient features that should be included in your portal.

- *Who participates in the process?* Consider customers, suppliers, channel partners, and third-party service providers as well as internal staff. Since portals are built on standard Internet protocols it is now much easier to integrate services across departments and organizations than it was when mainframes and client/server systems were predominant.
- *What are the high-level steps in the process?* How is the process initiated? What determines the next step in the process? What information is needed at each step? Answering these questions defines the skeleton of the process.
- *What are the dependencies between steps in the process?* Workflow processes are organized around discrete steps that often depend on the successful completion of other steps. Map these out at a high level along with the participants and the steps.
- *What business rules govern the process?* For the purpose of portal design, we do not need to understand fine-grained business rules enforced within

applications, for example, rules for determining the legitimacy of an insurance claim. For our purpose, we need to understand rules that govern the flow of information between applications. We also need to address administrative support and rules that govern the logging of operational information about the portal.

- *What systems and applications support the process?* Again, we do not need to know fine-grained details about applications, but we must know which applications support the business process we are modeling as well as their security and data interchange requirements.

- *How often is the process executed?* High-volume operations, such as those supporting claims processing, require a different design than low-volume, collaborative operations.

- *Which steps can be eliminated or combined in a portal-driven workflow?* Organizations have justified the entire cost of a portal just by eliminating paper reports or the need for postal mail.

For large projects, the Unified Modeling Language (UML) or other modeling methodology should be used to frame and document requirements. In many cases, however, basic diagrams with paragraph-length annotations are the best way to describe a process and have it reviewed and verified by others in the organization. These requirements do not have to lead to long reports with detailed minutia. The goal at this point is to understand the basic business requirements and develop a portal framework to support those needs. Remember, the fine-grained business requirements are the most likely to change over time, especially when you have an eye to combining steps and redesigning process flows. The portal framework you design should not have to change with changes in low-level business processes.

## Gathering Requirements for Collaboration Portals

Collaboration requires both formal and ad hoc information-sharing tools. Formal methods center on document management systems that provide centralized, often hierarchical storage for content. These systems also support metadata attributes and advanced search features. Ad hoc collaboration tools support less structured communications with threaded discussions, community areas, Web logs, and the ability to annotate formal documents with comments. Not everything we need to do our jobs is written down. Sometimes we just need to get answers to specific questions or want to discuss a problem with someone who has dealt with similar situations. Expert directories are a specialized type of formal collaboration and should be included in collaboration portals.

For formal collaboration tools, consider the following questions.

- *What content is accessible?* Only information in document and content management systems? Will shared directories be included? Are public e-mail folders accessible?
- *What are the subgroups of users?* Engineers, sales staff, and line-of-business managers are all interested in products but in different ways. Understand the different needs of these groups so they can find the content they need as well as others who can support their work.
- *What are the privacy concerns of portal users?* This is especially problematic if semipublic (at least semipublic to the organization) repositories like public e-mail folders and group directories are searchable through an enterprise search system in a portal.

For ad hoc collaboration tools, consider the following questions.

- *Are communities open or closed?* Engineers may want open discussion groups to encourage feedback from front-line production managers while managers might want closed communities hosted by the human resources department to discuss techniques for handling personnel issues.
- *How is content reviewed?* Can anyone add content to collaborative areas? Are discussion threads moderated? The integrity of content is essential to building users' trust. If users suspect case studies and white papers gloss over difficult implementation details or avoid frank discussions of mistakes, the value of that content diminishes.

For expert directories, consider the following questions.

- *How can people connect with experts?* In many cases, having the e-mail or phone number of the author of a document or message is enough to find someone who can help with a problem. In other cases, you may need specific information about skills and project experience. Consider linking from documents and messages to the author's entry in an expert directory.
- *Who is included in the directory?* The basic criteria are that an expert has specialized knowledge or experience and is willing to share that experience. Beware of potential problems. For example, will listing someone as an

"expert" change his or her standing relative to collective bargaining? Is the vice president of sales really an expert on every sales channel, and if not, will he or she be offended if not listed as an expert?

- *How will the directory be maintained?* In large organizations, a centralized human resources system can seed and update the directory. Also consider governance issues. Who gets to update a directory entry?
- *How should expertise be measured and evaluated?* Should managers survey users of the expert directory to get confidential feedback on experts and use those results to determine who remains in the directory? Should experts be reviewed like books at Amazon.com? Peer reviews are valued services at many Web sites, but do they fit with your organizational culture? Tread lightly in this area.

Asking these questions about processes and collaboration will no doubt lead to a plethora of other more detailed, organization-specific questions. Once you have answers, it is time to move to the design step.

## Designing the Portal

When designing a portal you must consider both technical and organizational issues. We can frame portal design around four broad dimensions:

1. Function
2. Organization
3. Information architecture
4. Enterprise architecture

Much of the information needed to address the function and organization dimensions is discovered following the requirements gathering framework outlined above. We address the information architecture and enterprise architecture dimensions for the first time in the design step.

### Function

The function dimension deals with how processes and collaboration are implemented within the portal. These tasks are highly dependent on the requirements gathered in the first step and on the portal software selected for your system [Sullivan 2003a and 2003b]. In general, you will have to answer the following questions.

- *How are authentication and authorization managed?* This is closely tied to directories, single sign-on systems, and other elements of the enterprise architecture dimension.
- *How are content repositories integrated with the portal?* Of course, multiple repositories can each have a Web interface, but how are search and classification implemented across repositories?
- *How are data exchange services modeled?* For example, will you need custom XML schemes or will you use industry-standard schemes to move data between deeply integrated applications?
- *How are user accounts provisioned?* Is that service provided by a separate enterprise group or is it a function for portal administrators to manage?
- *How are workflows implemented?* As with search systems, constituent applications may have embedded workflow systems, but how will you manage cross-application workflow? Does the enterprise already use a middleware system that can support this?

The function dimension is defined by more questions that you must address as your implementation proceeds. As we'll discuss later in the chapter, you do not have to implement all these components at once, but you do need to design the framework before you start deploying.

## Organization

The organization dimension addresses the softer, people-oriented issues that portals raise. Sometimes technically inclined designers discount organizational issues as either outside their area of expertise or not really as important as the technical challenges. Don't kid yourself. A technically superb portal is a waste of time and resources if it is not used, and if organizational challenges are not met, people will not use the portal. Plan for three core organizational issues once the requirements are defined:

- Privacy and confidential information
- Governance
- Adoption

Each of these is discussed briefly below.

*Privacy and Confidential Information*

Privacy is especially important when enterprise search is included in the portal. The problem is exemplified by e-mail.

E-mail is the third rail of enterprise search—do not touch unless you are ready for a shock. Regardless of official corporate policies that all e-mail is the property of the organization and subject to monitoring, e-mail folders are private spaces as much as offices and cubicles. Yes, we all understand our employers can come into our offices and search through our drawers—but they don't, at least not without good reason. Private space, whether physical or digital, must be respected within an organization. Develop a policy that describes what content is included in enterprise search systems and accessible through the portal. By all means, include public e-mail folders; just make sure that users understand those folders are indexed for search and that the appropriate access controls are put in place.

The same principles apply to other content made available through a portal. Users should at least know what information is now widely available. Also, consider the possibility that portals provide easy access to a broad range of information that when pieced together reveals confidential or protected information. Externally, gathering competitive intelligence on other businesses is much easier now with Web search engines than it was prior to the Internet. Similarly, enterprise search could remove barriers to information gathering that protected sensitive information in the past.

*Governance*

Privacy is one example of a governance issue; there are more. During the design step, begin laying the groundwork for governing the maintenance and evolution of the portal. Consider the following questions.

- *How will architecture issues be decided?* Architecture is itself a multidimensional element of a portal and its environment. In some organizations, a portal is the first broadly used application and therefore raises new issues about department-level versus enterprise-level controls.
- *Who will define content taxonomies, facets, and other metadata standards?* The specific answers to questions about what metadata attributes to use fall within the rubric of information architecture, but who makes those decisions is a question of governance. In most cases, a federated model of governance is best for balancing the needs of the organization with the requirements of individuals, teams, and departments.

- *Who determines access to processes?* When user access is application specific it is easy to determine who decides and grants access. Portals allow for deep integration between applications and require changes in the model.

How well a portal is governed can determine how well it is adopted.

### Adoption

Issues around adoption are central to a portal's success and were detailed in Chapter 4. Here we will simply note that adoption should be addressed during the design stage, right along with the technical issues. Do not wait until after implementation to address this factor—it may not be too late then, but it could slow the growth of the portal user base.

With a handle on the functional and organizational aspects of portal design, it is time to turn to the architectural components.

## Information Architecture

The information architecture of a portal defines how users move about and use the portal. It provides a sense of context and services for users. When working on the information architecture, consider the following questions.

- *What subsites or neighborhoods do you expect in the portal?* These could be functional neighborhoods, for example, areas for sales personnel or engineers. There could be project-oriented or department neighborhoods. You may also develop general resource neighborhoods with utilities and content of broad interest.
- *How will the portal provide a sense of context?* The presence of active links that show a user's location within a hierarchy is one method. The use of collapsing and expanding navigation menus (often in the left margin of a portal page) is another method.
- *How can the users personalize the portal?* Users should be able to specify specific interests, choose utilities, and join open communities. The portal should also provide access to tools based on roles. For example, financial analysts, engineers, and statisticians would have job-specific tools readily available from a toolbar or menu by virtue of information stored in an enterprise directory.
- *How can users browse and navigate from place to place?* This is especially important when a user knows something is "out there" somewhere but does not know how to effectively search for it.

- *How can users target their searches to prevent an overwhelming number of hits?* Metadata and easy-to-use advanced search forms are key to this.
- *How will users find specific applications or reports?* An application metadata directory should be created to help users find what they want.

Information architecture is closely linked to both governance issues and enterprise architecture.

### Enterprise Architecture

Accommodating enterprise architecture issues is one of the most time-consuming and resource-intensive parts of a portal implementation. It is difficult to overestimate the effort required to fully address these issues. This book cannot possibly cover all the topics you may face with your implementation, but here are a few you should be sure to cover.

- *Single sign-on:* Understand how single sign-on works in your environment. Determine whether you will need custom code to support legacy applications. Decide whether you will use both role-based and rule-based access controls and if so, how they will be managed.
- *Network security:* How does the introduction of the portal change your network security? Are you opening new ports on your firewalls? Do you need a virtual private network to link geographically separated offices?
- *Network capacity:* How will the portal affect network traffic? Will enterprise search systems crawl content over slow network connections? If so, how will it affect throughput? Will there be an initial period of high network demand when content is loaded into a portal repository?
- *Server platforms:* Where will the portal be hosted? If an outside provider is used, how will it support integration with other systems? What operating systems should be used?
- *Scalability:* What is the architecture of the portal software? Does the portal support a distributed configuration?
- *Application integration:* What middleware, if any, will be used? Are data exchanges in real time or batch?
- *Redundancy and failover:* Is the portal expected to be up 24/7? What is the window to correct a failure and roll over to a different server?
- *Backup and recovery:* The portal and its constituent document management systems will require backup and recovery plans.

Since a portal touches many other parts of an enterprise's IT infrastructure, its deployment must be carefully planned.

## Assessing the Return on Investment

You should make preliminary ROI calculations (see Chapter 5) once you have gathered requirements. When the design step is done, reassess the ROI calculations. At that point you should have more detailed cost estimates and should be able to better assess the savings realized by the portal. Perhaps most importantly, you will understand the technical and organizational hurdles that remain (there are always a few).

With the new numbers in hand, make your best assessment about whether or not to continue the project. If the numbers still favor a portal, move to the implementation step.

## Incrementally Implementing and Adapting the Portal

The last step of the process is implementation. After completing the previous three steps you have a firm understanding of your requirements, a solid design for meeting those requirements and fitting the portal into the existing enterprise architecture, and an assessment of the ROI. The implementation phase should be done incrementally with a rollout of features and applications as they become available.

Ideally, the first components should support some level of collaboration since as many as 70% of portal users cite that as the most significant benefit of portals [Palmer 2003]. It should also incorporate basic elements of information architecture, such as subsites, global navigation, and search systems. Taxonomies and rich metadata searching should be introduced in the second round of implementation. The portal should also introduce applications early in the deployment. Users should have the ability to make modest customizations early in the process. After the portal is implemented, monitor activity and survey users about their satisfaction and unmet expectations. This can provide valuable information to guide the next iteration of deployment. Following this strategy will allow you to deploy the first-round portal with a breadth of services without focusing too heavily on application integration, taxonomy development, and other time-consuming factors.

Two caveats. First, do not be so concerned with showing incremental improvement that you sacrifice on design. It is too easy to focus on delivering feature after feature without giving due consideration to overall design. The portal will suffer in the long run, and in the end you will end up addressing design issues anyway. Second, the best practices in this book should be considered guides for designing your portal. The case studies reflect some of the best portal design efforts in industry and government. They do not, however, replace the hard work that lies ahead for anyone designing their own portal. Do not be lulled into thinking that someone can download a list of best practices, lock a group of stakeholders in a room for a few days, and come up with a functional portal. If life were that easy you would not be reading books like this. Each of the proven portals described in this book succeeded because the designers and developers followed best practices and continuously worked to improve the product for their users, sometimes over a period of several years. Fortunately, we now have a repeatable process for creating more proven portals.

## Conclusion

The key to designing a successful portal is to use the same process that has lead to other successful software development projects. Understanding business requirements, developing a sound design, validating the value of the project, and incrementally implementing the portal while making adjustments based on user feedback are proven techniques. Following them will not guarantee success, but the process will help you avoid many potential pitfalls.

## References

Palmer, Nathaniel. 2003. "Portals and Collaboration." *AIIM E-DOC Magazine,* January/February. Accessed in June 2003 at *http://www.edocmagazine.com/vault _articles.asp?ID=25764&header=e_columns_header.gif.*

Sullivan, Dan. 2003a. "Vendor Evaluations Part 1: Functional Requirements." *DM Review,* February. Accessed in June 2003 at *http://www.dmreview.com/master .cfm?NavID=198&EdID=6285.*

———. 2003b. "Vendor Evaluations Part 2: Designing an In-House Evaluation." *DM Review,* March. Accessed in June 2003 at *http://www.dmreview.com/master .cfm?NavID=198&EdID=6401.*

# Bibliography

Aiken, Matt, and Dan Sullivan. 2002. "Best Practices in Enterprise Information Portal Adoption: 5 Key Drivers." *DM Review*, November. Accessed in June 2003 at *http://www.dmreview.com/master.cfm?NavID=55&EdID=5963*.

Baveja, Sarabjit Singh. 2000. "Making the Most of Customers." *The Industry Standard*, March 6. Accessed in June 2003 at *http://www.thestandard.com/article/0,1902,11978,00.html*.

Bernard, Allen. 2003. "Planning Key to Portal ROI." *Datamation*, February 14. Accessed in June 2003 at *http://itmanagement.earthweb.com/entdev/article.php/1584481*.

Bourke, Tony. 2001. *Server Load Balancing*. Cambridge, MA: O'Reilly.

Britton, Chris. 2001. *IT Architectures and Middleware: Strategies for Building Large, Integrated Systems*. Boston, MA: Addison-Wesley.

CIOview. 1999–2003. "Financial Primer: How to Calculate ROI, NPV, Payback and IRR." Accessed in June 2003 at *http://www.cioview.com/resource_whitepapers_financial.asp*.

Code, W. F., J. T. Kruelen, V. Krishna, and W. S. Spangler. 2002. "The Integration of Business Intelligence and Knowledge Management." *IBM Systems Journal* 41(4). Accessed in June 2003 at *http://www.almaden.ibm.com/software/km/bi/BIKM.pdf*.

Datamonitor. 2002. *Single Sign-On: Enterprise Access Made Secure and Easy.* Accessed in June 2003 at *http://www3.ca.com/Files/IndustryAnalystReports/SSO.pdf.*

eGain Communications Corporation. 2002. "Case Study: Quick & Reilly and eGain." Accessed in February 2003 at *http://www.egain.com/.*

Finklestein, Clive. 2001. "Enterprise Portal Success." *DM Review*, March. Accessed in June 2003 at *http://www.dmreview.com/master.cfm?NavID=198&EdID=3083.*

Kimball, Ralph, Laura Reeves, Margy Ross, and Warren Thornthwaite. 1998. *The Data Warehouse Lifecycle Toolkit.* New York: Wiley.

Kramer, David Ben-Gal, and Bill Brendler. 2001. "Sticky Conversations in Customer Care." *Intelligent Enterprise*, January 30. Accessed in June 2003 at *http://www.intelligentcrm.com/feature/010130/featJan1.shtml.*

Krug, Steve, and Roger Black. 2000. *Don't Make Me Think: A Common Sense Approach to Web Usability.* Indianapolis, IN: Que.

Levene, Mark, and George Loizou. 1999. "Navigation in Hypertext Is Easy Only Sometimes." Accessed in June 2003 at *http://www.dcs.bbk.ac.uk/~mark/download/htext.pdf.*

Linthicum, David S. 2001. "Making EAI Scale." *Intelligent Enterprise*, April 16. Accessed in June 2003 at *http://www.intelligenteai.com/feature/010416/linthicum.shtml.*

Luedtke, Joseph. 2003. "The Lexicon of BI." *Intelligent Enterprise*, May 13. Accessed in June 2003 at *http://www.intelligententerprise.com/030513/608feat3_1.shtml.*

Martin, Ray. 1997. "Internal Rate of Return Revisited." Accessed in June 2003 at *http://members.tripod.com/~Ray_Martin/DCF/nr7aa003.html.*

McCormick, Garvin. 2001. "IT Spending Slowing, Not Stopping." *Datamation*, May 24. Accessed in June 2003 at *http://itmanagement.earthweb.com/ecom/article/0,,11952_772981,00.html.*

Moss, Larissa T., and Shaku Atre. 2003. *Business Intelligence Roadmap: The Complete Project Lifecycle for Decision-Support Applications.* Boston, MA: Addison-Wesley.

Nielsen, Jakob. 1999. *Designing Web Usability: The Practice of Simplicity.* Indianapolis, IN: New Riders.

Palmer, Nathaniel. 2003. "Portals and Collaboration." *AIIM E-DOC Magazine*, January/February. Accessed in June 2003 at *http://www.edocmagazine.com/vault_articles.asp?ID=25764&header=e_columns_header.gif.*

Pirolli, Peter, Stuart K. Card, and Mija M. Van der Wege. (Year not stated.) "The Effect of Information Scent on Searching Information Visualization of Large Tree Structures." Accessed in June 2003 at *http://www.inxight.com/pdfs/PARCstudy.pdf.*

Plumtree Software. 2003. "No Empty Portals! Workshop Series." Accessed in June 2003 at *http://www.plumtree.com/reg/fs/noemptyportals/.*

————. 2002. "Corporate Portal ROI." Accessed in June 2003 at *http://www.plumtree.com/webforms/process/file_opener.asp?docname=ROIWhitePaper_April2002.pdf.*

Red Hat. 2002. "Customer Profile: Siemens: ICN ShareNet." Accessed in June 2003 at *http://www.redhat.com/software/rhea/customers/siemens/.*

Reichheld, Fredrick F., and Phil Schefter. 2000. "E-loyalty: Your Secret Weapon on the Web." *Harvard Business Review,* July–August. Accessed in June 2003 at *http://harvardbusinessonline.hbsp.harvard.edu/b01/en/common/item_detail.jhtml?id=5181.*

Rossi, Gustov, Daniel Schwabe, and Fernando Lyardet. (Year not stated.) "Improving Web Information Systems with Navigational Patterns." Accessed in June 2003 at *http://www8.org/w8-papers/5b-hypertext-media/improving/improving.html.*

Schmarzo, Bill. 2002. "The Promise of Decision Support." *Intelligent Enterprise,* December 5. Accessed in June 3003 at *http://www.intelligententerprise.com/021205/601warehouse1_1.shtml.*

Smith, Mark. 2002. "Strategic Assessment Guide." *Intelligent Enterprise,* October 1. Accessed in June 2003 at *http://www.intelligententerprise.com/online_only/saguide2002/saguide.shtml.*

Sullivan, Dan. 2003a. "Vendor Evaluations Part 1: Functional Requirements." *DM Review,* February. Accessed in June 2003 at *http://www.dmreview.com/master.cfm?NavID=198&EdID=6285.*

————. 2003b. "Vendor Evaluations Part 2: Designing an In-House Evaluation." *DM Review,* March. Accessed in June 2003 at *http://www.dmreview.com/master.cfm?NavID=198&EdID=6401.*

————. 2002. "Visions of Intelligence." *Intelligent Enterprise,* May 28. Accessed in June 2003 at *http://www.intelligententerprise.com/020528/509feat2_1.shtml.*

————. 2002a. "Ensuring Adoption of Information Portals." *DM Review,* August. Accessed in June 2003 at *http://www.dmreview.com/master.cfm?NavID=55&EdID=5569.*

————. 2002b. "When the Emperor Has No Clothes." *DM Review*, September. Accessed in June 2003 at *http://www.dmreview.com/master.cfm?NavID =55&EdID=5676.*

————. 2001. *Document Warehousing and Text Mining.* New York: Wiley.

Sullivan, Danny. 2001. "WebTop Search Rage Study." Accessed in June 2003 at *http://searchenginewatch.com/sereport/article.php/2163351.*

Tannenbaum, Adrienne. 2002. *Metadata Solutions: Using Metamodels, Repositories, XML, and Enterprise Portals to Generate Information on Demand.* Boston, MA: Addison-Wesley.

Taylor, Laura. 2002. "Understanding Single Sign-On." *Intranet.com*, May 28. Accessed in June 2003 at *http://www.intranetjournal.com/articles/200205/se _05_28_02a.html.*

TheBrain Technologies. 2002. "Center Partners: Improving Call Handle Times and Agent Best Practices." Received via e-mail from TheBrain.

Thomsen, Erik. 1997. *OLAP Solutions: Building Multidimensional Information Systems.* New York: Wiley.

Wenger, Etienne. 1999. *Communities of Practice.* New York: Cambridge University Press.

Wu, Jonathan. 2003a. "Calculating ROI for Business Intelligence Projects Part 1." Accessed in June 2003 at *http://www.datawarehouse.com/iknowledge/articles/ article.cfm?ContentID=936.*

————. 2003b. "Calculating ROI for Business Intelligence Projects Part 2." Accessed in June 2003 at *http://www.datawarehouse.com/iknowledge/articles/ article.cfm?ContentID=937.*

————. 2003c. "Calculating ROI for Business Intelligence Projects Part 3." Accessed in June 2003 at *http://www.datawarehouse.com/iknowledge/articles/ article.cfm?ContentID=940.*

# Index

Page numbers followed by *f* and *t* indicate figures and tables, respectively.

# informIT